A Guide to Help Lawyers, Law Students, and Business Professionals Develop Cross-Cultural Competence

By Scott Fruehwald

This book is intended for educational and informational purposes only.

Copyright 2021

All Rights Reserved

ISBN: 9798536893012

Table of Contents

Introduction	1
I. Preliminary Questions: Cross-Cultural Competence	3
II. An Introduction to Cross-Cultural Competence	7
III. Motivating Yourself for Cross-Cultural Competence	13
IV. Discovering Differences Among Cultures	22
V. Cross-Cultural Competence for Lawyers and Business Professionals	28
VI. Cross-Cultural Competence in Business	52
Reflection Questions	56
Conclusion	57

A Guide to Help Lawyers, Law Students, and Business Professionals Develop Cross-Cultural Competence

My grandparents never traveled. They were born in Evansville, Indiana, and they lived most of their lives in Louisville, Kentucky. They never went far from their home on Camden Avenue near downtown Louisville. Neither of them drove a car; my grandfather took a bus to work at the L & N Railroad. Their social circle was limited, and they didn't interact a lot with people from other cultures.

100 years later, things have changed dramatically. I have traveled extensively in North America, Europe, and the Caribbean. My law students come from all over the country and all over the world. They come from all economic classes and a multitude of ethnic groups. Even on a day-to-day basis, I interact with people from throughout the world and different cultures. I need to be able to interact with all people.

As the above illustrates, today, we live in a diverse world, and cross-cultural competence is important for everyone. This is especially true for lawyers and business professionals. As one author has written, "No matter a lawyer's practice area, it is imperative that each lawyer possess the ability to interact and communicate effectively with people from other cultures."[1] This is why I have written this book.

A key part of being a lawyer or business professional is the ability to deal with others. Part of this ability is the recognition that the people you will deal with come from many different cultures and backgrounds. We are all human, but there is a great deal of variation among humans.

People from all cultural groups need cross-cultural training.[2] No one culture is more culturally sensitive than another. As one scholar has written, "We recognized that intercultural learning was important for all students."[3]

"Cross-cultural competence" is the "ability to understand people from different cultures and engage with them effectively."[4] It involves "'the ability to function effectively in another culture', consisting of three interdependent dimensions: 1) an affective dimension (personality traits and attitudes), 2) a cognitive dimension (how individuals acquire and categorize cultural knowledge), and a communicative, behavioral dimension (being an effective communicator)."[5] In other words, attitudes, knowledge, and skills.

Most importantly, it requires an individual "to step outside his/her cultural boundary, to make the strange familiar and the familiar strange, and to act on that change of perspective."[6]

More specifically,

> Cultural competency is not about conforming one's personal beliefs or opinions to a politically correct external standard. Rather, it is about actions. It means recognizing that our clients are not fungible and that every one of them brings to the representation a set of values, beliefs and other cultural norms that affect the client's view of their problems and how they should be addressed. Whether or not there is an ethical obligation of culturally competence, it is a practical necessity in modern law practice if we are committed to equal justice and high-quality client service.[7]

More specifically for lawyers, it is a lawyer's "ability to develop knowledge, skills, and values to enable effective representation and communication with individuals from a different race, ethnicity, gender, sexual orientation, age or cultural background."[8]

While cross-cultural competence has been an essential part of medical education and business for years,[9] it is not usually part of legal education.[10] However, it is essential to attorney competence, and it can give practitioners a competitive edge.[11] In fact, one could argue that cross-culture competence is required under Model Rule 1.1: Competence ("A lawyer shall provide competent representation to a client. Competent representation requires the legal knowledge, skill, thoroughness and preparation reasonably necessary for the representation.").[12]

Cross-cultural competence is also important in business. As one might expect, lack of cross-cultural competence can cause international business failure.[13] Such problems can include 1) expatriate failure (managers returning home early due to the inability to function in a foreign culture, which has been estimated at 40-55%), 2) the poor choice of a local partner, 3) the inability to effectively manage a foreign merger, acquisition or joint venture, and 4) a poor understanding of the local economic, political, and sociocultural environments.[14]

Here is an example how lack of cross-cultural competence caused a significant problem for a business operating in China:[15]

For years, the Chinese branch of a major European-based multinational pharmaceutical company saved significant money by submitting its proposals for the approval of new medicines in English to the Chinese government, even though the "rule" stated the application should be in Chinese. To write the application in Chinese would be very expensive (requiring new computers, keyboards, software, etc). After sometime, the company changed one of its top people in China (who had established excellent relationships with Chinese government officials) without informing or consulting with the Chinese authorities. The Chinese were offended, and mandated that the company now submit all documents in Chinese (at great expense and lost time). If the company had the cultural intelligence (CQ) to understand the importance of long-standing relationships in the Chinese culture, they undoubtedly would have taken the time to overlap the new and current executives and so that the current executive could make a formal introduction of his re-placement.

Part I of this book will evaluate the current state of your cross-cultural competence. Part II will introduce you to cross-cultural competence and help you develop some general cross-competence skills. Part III will explain how to motivate yourself for cross-cultural competence. Part IV will help you discover differences among cultures. Part V will help you develop specific skills for law or business. Part VI will cover problems that are especially relevant to businesses. This Guide will end with wrap-up exercises.

I. Preliminary Questions: Cross-Cultural Competence

The purpose of these questions is to help you determine your current cross-cultural competence and cause you to start thinking about cross-cultural competence before you dig into this book. They are also intended to make you think about yourself. As one writer has asserted, "To become good cross-cultural lawyers, students must first become aware of the significance of culture on themselves."[16]

Preliminary Questions

1. Are you open to new things? Are you interested in other cultures? Are you interested in foreign cultures? Are you interested in other cultures in your country?
2. Think of a foreign country you are particularly interested in, but have not traveled to. What do you know about this culture? The people? The history? The government? The food? The art? The music? The customs? The religion? How did you learn about this culture? How would you do if you traveled to this country by yourself? How would you do if you had to travel to this country on business? Do you think you would do okay in this country if you had to live there a few years?
3. Have you ever traveled to a foreign country? How was your experience? What problems did you have to deal with? Did you try to speak some of the language? How was the food? Did you try to experience the culture? Did you prepare for your trip? Do you wish that you had prepared more? What did you think of the natives of the country? Were they friendly to you? If not, was it their fault or your fault?
4. Let's switch to other cultures within your country. I am going to use the United States since most of this book's readers will be from there, but you can adopt the questions to any culture. Write down the main characteristics the culture you grew up in. (White, Black, Latino, Asian-American, Northern, Southern, Western, lower class, middle class, Catholic, etc.) (before you can learn another culture, you must understand your own.)
5. As you were growing up, did you interact with people from other cultures? At school? Outside school? At church? At public events? Other places?
6. As you were growing up, did you have problems dealing with other cultures or people from other cultures? How did you deal with these problems? Could you have done a better job dealing with these problems? Did you find people from other cultures strange? Did you try to get to know them?
7. Think about the various cultures in this country. Black, Latino, White, Asian-American, Middle Eastern, Protestant, Catholic, Southern, Californian.

What do you know about these cultures? Do you want to know more? Do you need to know more to function effectively in this country?
8. Think of the attitudes of your parents, your teachers, and other adults to different cultures as you were growing up? How did these attitudes influence you–positively or negatively?
9. Are all people in a race, ethnic group, or religion the same? Think about how many types of Latino groups there are in this country? How are these groups similar or different?
10. How does regionalism affect racial culture?
11. How does religion affect ethnic groups?
12. How does socio-economic class affect ethnic groups?
13. Take an ethnic group in your country and compare it to your ethnic group. Do the same for race, religion, socio-economic class and region.

Preliminary Questions: Dealing with Other People

How you deal with other people is an important part of cross-cultural competence. These questions are intended to start you thinking about how you deal with other people. Be honest; no one else will see your answers.

1. Are you good at dealing with other people?
2. Did you get into fights when you were in elementary school? How did you get along with your friends in high school? Do you have a lot of close friends today?
3. How did you get along with your teachers in high school? How did you get along with your professors in college? When you received a bad grade on an exam or a paper did you blame the teacher? How did you interact with your parents while you were growing up? What values did your parents instill in you?
4. How would you change your past interactions with people if you could?
5. What is the worst thing you have ever done while interacting with another person?
6. Are you an introvert or an extrovert? How has this affected your life?
7. Who were your role models growing up? Looking back, were these role models the best you could have had?
8. Have you had much interaction with people from other cultures?

9. How do you interact with people from other cultures? Do you treat them all the same? Do you feel uncomfortable when interacting with people from other cultures?
10. Do you stereotype individuals from other cultures? Why do you do this? Do you see the problems that stereotyping causes?
11. Have you had difficulties with persons from other cultures at work? At school? At events? In public? Who was responsible for these problems?
12. If you saw a person from your culture cheat on an exam would you turn them in? If you saw a person from another culture cheat on an exam, would you turn them in? Were your answers the same?
13. Think about a person you know well who is from a foreign country. How are your interactions with them? Do you treat them the same or differently than a person from your country? Why?
14. Think about a person you know well from another racial or ethnic group? How are your interactions with them? Do you treat them the same as people from your racial or ethnic group? Why? Do the same for other religions, socio-economic groups, regional groups, and genders?
15. Do you consciously think about your moral dilemmas? How do you solve moral problems?
16. Do you think about how your actions affect others?
17. Do you listen to your inner voice? Do you learn from your mistakes?

True or False

1. I am more likely to vote for a candidate of my race than a candidate from another racial group.
2. I make fun of people with foreign accents.
3. I make fun of people who dress strangely.
4. I think "my culture is superior to all others."
5. I don't understand people from a particular ethnic group.
6. I sometimes think "why doesn't everybody in France speak English." (or, something similar).
7. I sometimes ask why people from a specific group have such strange customs.

8. I have thought "why do we have that public holiday. Only people from a small group celebrate it."
9. I have thought "why do people from that group listen to such awful music."
10. I have thought "poor people are poor through their own fault."
11. I have thought "all rich people cheated to get where they are."
12. My culture's value system is the best.
13. I criticize cultures who don't treat women equally to mine.
14. I like to make fun of people, but they laugh with me.
15. I consider other people's feelings when making jokes.
16. I consider other people's feelings when speaking.
17. I believe that people should have a tough shell just like me.
18. I criticize cultures who practice female circumcision.
19. I am interested in learning other languages.
21. I am interested about other cultures.
22. I am curious.
23. I respect people from other generations.

Note: Cross-cultural competence requires that you don't treat your culture as superior (cultural humility). However, criticizing other cultures is not always bad because some of those practices hurt others. Can you spot these in the above list?

II. An Introduction to Cross-Cultural Competence

This section will introduce you to cross-culture competence.

Professors Hamilton and Maleska have developed a four-part model of cross-cultural competence growth: "(1) lack of awareness, (2) recognition, (3) conscious implementation, and (4) proficiency."[17] Those in the first stage "reflect[] ignorance of the role that culture plays in one's interactions with others." In the second stage, "one acknowledges their lack of cross-cultural competency, but may be unsure of how to develop it. Indeed, someone at this stage may notice the role culture plays, reflect on how their own culture affects decisions and begin to see the need to develop cross-cultural competency." In the third stage, "one takes an initial affirmative step toward developing cross-cultural competency in a specific area by refraining from making on-the-spot judgments in unfamiliar situations." In the final stage, "a person has become educated in the particular culture and could fairly be considered as cross-culturally competent in that area. A person at this stage is able to interact freely and genuinely within another culture and understands that culture's differing viewpoints and customs."

Here are seven strategies for developing cross-cultural competence:[18]

1. **Know yourself—and how you're different**: Be aware that you see the world in a certain way because of your background, personal history, and culture. Everybody brings their own perspective to a situation. Understanding how others perceive you can give you an advantage.
2. **Know the value of a little cultural understanding**: Understand why it's important to learn even a little about a culture. Focus on what you need to know to accomplish your goals while you're abroad. Don't feel you need to know 'everything' about a culture. That frees you up to research the things you're really interested in.
3. **Frame intercultural interactions as opportunities to learn**: Expect to continue to learn new things about a culture the whole time you are in it. Treat every new tidbit you digest as a tool to learn more.
4. **Pay attention to surprises**: Be alert to actions that you find puzzling. Like a good scientist, inquire into the cause of unexpected behavior. If something or somebody offends you or gets offended, that's a good cue to ask "why did they do that?" This is one of several metacognitive strategies or "mental habits" you can use to gain deep insight into new cultures.
5. **Test your knowledge**: Expect that only a small amount of what have been told about the culture is true. If you think you know something about a culture, ask a native. They'll be amused and you might learn a thing or two.
6. **Reflect on your experiences**: Continue to think about your experiences after they happened. There's value in doing a play-by-play analysis, especially if something about it just gives you a 'weird feeling.' (See point 4.)

7. **Adapt what you express and how you express it**: Use your understanding of a culture to decide how to express yourself to accomplish your goals. Plan how you want to say things. Importantly, adapt the strategies you use to fit you own personality. Being genuine is key. Pretending to be someone you're not doesn't win you any points.

Exercise: Cross-Cultural Competence Strategies

1. Which of the above strategies do you already use in your interactions with people from other cultures? Which ones do you need to develop?

It should be noted that cross-cultural training can often be emotionally difficult for many students and even self-learners.[19] One study concluded:

> Why, indeed, would these course sessions leave residents so unsettled? First, depending upon their backgrounds, biographies, and personal inclinations, some residents were more comfortable than others in discussing the clinical implications of racial/ethnic and cultural difference. Broadly speaking, residents whose background could be described as "non-mainstream" generally were more comfortable talking about these issues and often were more sophisticated in their reflections than those who described themselves simply as "white." Second, although the course touched upon deeply felt personal and professional concerns for "main-stream" and "non-mainstream" residents alike, the issues of greatest concern to these broadly defined groups tended to be quite different. Third, the structure of the course did not allow this range of voices, experiences, and anxieties to rise to the surface. Although several sessions were designed as workshops in "narrative medicine," they did not provide an atmosphere that allowed open discussion of feelings or reactions. Overall, the course offered few opportunities to

work through or learn from the differences among residents' reactions to the course content.[20]

Similarly, one participant in a in a cultural sensitivity course for psychiatry residents declared, "I feel like this door keeps getting swung wide open, a big huge gaping wound. People with a lot of feelings because they are of the minority race, or any number of minority races, let loose a whole bunch of feelings. And ... the majority either feel, like, horribly guilty, or accused, or criticized. Because it's not their intention to make people feel that way. And it's hard to examine what has happened. ... You know what I'm saying?"[21]

In other words, those who teach cross-cultural courses must be sensitive to the cultural backgrounds of all their students. Otherwise, they may produce more damage than good. Also, those who learn cross-cultural competence on their own need to understand that some things may be upsetting.

There are certain general skills you need to develop for cross-cultural competence. These include 1) developing interpersonal skills, 2) understanding body language, and 3) dealing with difficult people.

Developing Interpersonal Skills

Interpersonal skills are an important part of cross-cultural competence. Interpersonal skills can help you avoid cultural problems, even when you don't know much about the other person's culture.

Here are some interpersonal skills:

1. Create eye contact. (Unless you are dealing with an individual from a culture that avoids eye contact.)
2. Focus on developing your communication skills.
3. Develop your emotional intelligence.

4. Listen to how you are using your voice. (Tone, volume, do you talk too fast or too slow, clarity, etc.)
5. Consider your body language. (Is your body language open and welcoming, or does your body language indicate that you are closed to suggestions.)
6. Reflect on how you resolve conflicts.
7. Work on your problem-solving skills.
8. Take responsibility when appropriate.
9. Don't be a complainer.
10. Learn how to compromise.
11. Learn how to create trust.
12. Maintain your personal integrity.
13. Be dependable.
14. Develop patience.
15. Develop cross-cultural humility.
16. Be assertive, not aggressive.
17. Develop your teamwork skills.[22]

Exercises: Interpersonal Skills

1. Which of the items on the above list are you good at, and which ones are you poor at? Reflect on how you can improve your weak interpersonal skills.
2. Do you seek feedback at work or school?
3. Are you trusted by your employer? Does your employer think you are dependable?
4. Do you get along with your fellow employees? If not, why not?
5. How do you react to difficult situations at work or school?
6. Are you assertive or aggressive? Do you know the difference?

Here are some common examples of body language in American culture:

1. Slight raise of the eyebrows and a slight smile=trustworthiness.
2. Highly diluted eyeballs=desire.

3. Rapid blinking=distress or discomfort.
4. Eye contact=interest.
5. Biting the lips=worried or anxious.
6. Tight lips=distrust, distaste, disapproval.
7. Clinched fist=anger or solidarity.
8. Crossed arms=a person feels defensive, self-protective, or closed-off.
9. Clasping hands behind back=boredom, anxiety, or anger.
10. Hands on hips=person is in control or aggressiveness.
11. Rapidly tapping fingers or fidgeting=boredom, impatience, or frustration.
12. Cross-legs=person closed off or in need of privacy.
13. Open posture=friendliness, openness, and willingness.
14. Closed posture=hostility, unfriendliness, or anxiety.
15. Body turned away from you=disengaged, disinterested, or unhappy.
16. Touching face=dishonesty.
17. Open palms=trustworthiness, openness.[23]

Exercises: Body Language

1. Which elements of body language do you do well? Which one do you need to work on?
2. Does your body language express openness? What is the effect of closed body language?
3. As you watch television, pay attention to the actors; body language.

Dealing with Difficult People

An important part of cross-cultural competence is being able to deal with difficult people. I am sure there are many difficult people in your culture, but cultural differences add an addition element to the problem.
First, always consider that the difficult person might be undergoing a crisis that makes them difficult. For example, during a team building exercise, "Shortly after the day started, one of the team members seemed oblivious to the conversation and was tethered to her phone.

My client was furious. Not only did it feel disrespectful, but it also triggered her own insecurities about facilitating the group. But, at the morning break, my client asked (rather than accused) the team member if something was wrong. The woman explained that she was dealing with a serious family issue, and after their conversation, both agreed that this team member should leave to be with her family."[24]

Here are some techniques for dealing with difficult people:

1. Use kindness.
2. Be compassionate
3. Listen critically. (Explained below)
4. Stay calm. (Don't react with anger; don't react defensively.)
5. Explain your side.
6. Treat others with respect.
7. Control what you can.
8. Ignore them.
9. Don't be afraid of conflict.
10. Act professionally.
11. Try to determine why they are being difficult.
12. Find something in common. (Try to build a rapport.)[25]

With cross-cultural situations, there is an additional consideration: Is the person being difficult or is there a cultural difference?

Exercise: Dealing with Difficult People

1. How have you dealt with many difficult people in the past? Consider a particular situation and examine it in detail. How could you have handled the situation better?
2. How would you deal with a difficult person today?
3. What are the body language signs of difficult people?

III. Motivating Yourself for Cross-Cultural Competence

In order to be cross-culturally competent, you must want to be cross-culturally competent. This may be obvious, but self-motivation is often hard. This section will present the keys to self-motivation.

A. How Motivation Works

Motivation is "the personal investment that an individual has in reaching a desired state or outcome."[26] It is "the general answer to the question of 'why' we do what we do, especially why we do things that are hard to do."[27] In other words, how much are you willing to invest to achieve a goal?

Setting proper goals is the key to self-motivation. Setting goals gives you a reason to work hard. "I have this goal, and I am willing to do what it takes to achieve that goal." Setting goals also directs your attention on that goal (helps you focus on your goal).

There are three types of goals:

1) learning goals,
2) performance goals, and
3) work avoidance goals.

The most effective type of goals is learning goals, which are "goals directed at learning new knowledge or mastering a task or problem."[28] With learning goals, you concentrate on competence and the inherent facets of a task, learning for learning's sake, interest, challenge, and curiosity.[29]

Performance goals are "goals directed at demonstrating ability or doing especially well in relation to others," such as grades, or task goals (regarding assignments "as tasks to complete rather than opportunities to learn").[30] People who have performance goals want to protect their self-image and acquire status, recognition, and praise by appearing competent and intelligent.[31] When individuals with performance goals do not receive positive external feedback, they can become anxious, apathetic, or depressed, and they often adopt pro-crastination.[32]

Finally, work avoidance goals are getting "through with as little time and effort as possible."[33]

Three factors affect whether goals are motivating:

1) the subjective value of the goal,
2) the expectation for successful achievement of the goal ("expectancies"), and
3) whether the environment is supportive or unsupportive ("the environmental context").[34]

First, whether a goal is motivating depends on its value to you ("how much the goal is worth"), and how it compares to other goals.[35] Values are subjective and personal because humans learn to value things that engender positive emotions.[36] There are three types of value goals:

The first is attainment value, "which represents the satisfaction that one gains from mastery and accomplishment of a goal or task."[37] An example of attainment value is when a person devotes many hours to chess to master the game.
The second value is intrinsic value, "which represents the satisfaction that one gains from simply doing the task rather than from a particular outcome from a task."[38] An example of this value is when a person learns the cello just because they enjoy it.
Finally, instrumental value "represents the degree to which an activity or goal helps one accomplish other important goals, such as gaining what are usually referred to as extrinsic rewards."[39] Examples include studying economics to become a better lawyer or getting an M.B.A. at night to obtain a raise at work.

Second, the expectation for successful achievement of the goal comprises two parts:

1) outcome expectancies ("the belief a specific action will bring about the desired outcome") and

2) efficacy expectancies ("the belief that one is capable of identifying, organizing, initiating, and executing a course of action that will bring about the desired outcome").[40]

A positive outcome expectancy might be "if I work hard in this course I will get a good grade." A negative outcome expectancy, such as "no matter how hard I work in this class, I will get a C," can have significant consequences on a student's motivation, causing that student to give up.[41]

Connecting short-term goals with long-term goals can also create positive outcome expectancies.[42] For example, one might learn French to become more culturally competent and improve one's job prospects.

Here is a method of incrementally developing long-term goals:

(1) envision possible futures for yourself,
(2) conceptualize those futures as goals,
(3) construct a path for goal obtainment,
(4) make explicit connections between present educational activities and the valued future goals,
(5) discuss possible roadblocks and forks in your path,
(6) brainstorm strategies for managing imagined future obstacles, and
(7) interview successful adults from the community about their own strategies for reaching goals.[43]

Efficacy expectations (or self-efficacy) "affect human functioning by influencing the extent to which people are optimistic versus pessimistic, make resilient versus detrimental attributions for successes and failures, apply appropriate coping strategies for dealing with difficult situations, and persist in the face of challenges."[44] Efficacy expectations are important because "[s]tudents will not set and pursue a goal unless they feel confident that they can do what is needed to achieve it."[45] Students with high self-efficacy tend to be more engaged, work harder, and achieve more, as well as take harder courses.[46]

Efficacy expectations come mainly from a person's past successes ("mastery experiences") and failures.[47] "When students successfully achieve a goal and attribute their success to internal causes (for example, their own talents or abilities) or to controllable causes (for example, their own efforts or persistence) they are more likely to expect future success."[48] Efficacy expectations can also be obtained vicariously by observing others succeed and receive praise.[49] Other factors influencing efficacy expectations include: "(1) the student's current skill level, (2) the extent to which she has witnessed modeling from peers and teachers. . ., (3) verbal persuasion regarding the difficulty of the task, and (4) the student's current psychological state."[50] Negative efficacy expectations, (such as "last time I succeed by luck" or "I never will become a better student") can be particular damaging to motivation.

The final factor in motivating yourself through goals is whether the environment is supportive or unsupportive. An unsupporting environment can damage motivation, even in the presence of positive factors on the other elements.

Emotion can also affect motivation. Emotional motivators involve pleasure and pain.[51] Positive emotions help focus attention; individuals sustain effort and maintain capacity.[52] Negative emotions produce avoidance, such as avoiding a task that an individual thinks she is not good at (lack of self-efficacy).[53]

Interest (situational and personal) is a motivator that is usually associated with emotion, although it can have cognitive elements, too.[54] Situational interest comes from the environment, is produced by novelty ("sensory features that appear to draw our attention"), is generally based on positive emotions, and can be short- or long-term.[55] You can create situational interest by approaching learning in novel and exciting ways. On the other hand, personal interest (or curiosity) derives from our experiences.[56] It helps individuals work to long-term goals and helps sustain attention and persistence.[57] Developing your curiosity is the most important factor in becoming cross-culturally competent. As learning expert Daniel Willingham has declared, "Curiosity causes a brain state that amplifies learning."[58]

How you attribute success can also affect your motivation.[59] You are more likely to be motivated and succeed if you attribute success to controllable internal factors, like effort (a growth mindset).[60] On the other hand, if you attribute success or failure to external factors, such as luck, favoritism, or someone else, you destroy motivation.[61]

B. How to Motivate Yourself

Now that I've given you the theory behind self-motivation, let's discuss how you can motivate yourself. You can increase your motivation by

1) creating the subjective value of the goal,
2) creating the expectation for successful achievement of the goal, and
3) creating a positive learning environment.

Start with a goal. Goals can include "I will learn Spanish" or "I will learn how to play the violin." "I will write an excellent paper for English class." "I will become culturally-competent so I can work in Asia." "I will become culturally-competent so I can work in a law clinic." Make your goal as clear and detailed as possible.

Next, you want to create the subjective value for the goal. (Subjective means personal to you.) Preferably this will be a learning goal. Ask "what will I get from this goal?" ("I want to learn German because I want to be an international businessman.") Also, think about what accomplishing the goal will do for you. ("If I learn French this semester, I can study in Paris this summer.") Think how this goal will help with long-term goals. ("If I learn calculous, I can study advanced physics.") Finally, to make it a learning goal, try to be curious about the goal.

You also need to set goals for studying. Students are not motivated for studying by aimless study sessions. "What do I need to study tonight?" "What do I want to accomplish through this study session?"

You must also motivate yourself to learn skills. Learning is not just memorizing stuff; it is also about developing practical skills. Think how learning these skills will help you achieve your goals.

Setting long-term goals is also important. Here is a plan for creating long-term learning goals:

> First, individuals must establish an ideal self and a personal vision for the future (i.e., Who do you want to be?), which is based on developing an image of a desired future, fostering hope that one can achieve their goals, and identifying established strengths upon which the personal vision can be realized. Second, they must identify their "real self," which includes an honest assessment of strengths and weaknesses, and then compare it to their ideal self, or who they want to become. Third, they must devise a tailored learning plan, which establishes a set of personal standards that the individual needs to meet to "close the gap" between their real self and their ideal self. Fourth, they need to engage in activities that allow them to experiment or practice with new behaviors, thoughts, feelings, or perceptions. And finally, they must develop and maintain close, personal relationships with people who can help them move through these steps and toward their goal of realizing change.[62]

You must also create the expectation that you will successfully achieve your goal. You must develop self-efficacy–that your intellectual abilities are changeable if you use the sufficient effort and proper methods ("a growth mindset"), rather than unchangeable ("a fixed mindset").[63] (I discussed the theory of self-efficacy in detail above.) Focusing on learning goals, rather than performance goals, helps your self-efficacy because, with learning goals, achievement is measured against past performance and, thus, failure is less traumatic than when students have performance goals, such as getting a good grade or status.[64] You should frame "problems as surmountable and as a chance to practice and demonstrate specific skills, rather than threatening or barriers to success."[65]

You can also regulate your self-efficacy through self-efficacy "self-talk," where "[s]tudents engage in thoughts or subvocal statements aimed at influencing their efficacy for an ongoing academic task."[66] Such statements can include "You can learn to ski" or "You can write this philosophy paper." In fact, a recent study has shown that athletes that encourage themselves in the second person ("you") are more likely to triumph.[67]

You should also allow yourself opportunities to reflect.[68] Reflection from prior learning affects subsequent learning, particularly self-efficacy.[69] Reflection also helps you become invested in what you are doing, and it makes learning more interesting.

The final part of creating motivation is creating a favorable learning environment. While you are working on becoming culturally competent, do not surf the net, text friends, or stare out the window. The human mind has limited attention, and doing things other than learning wastes attention. Next, when studying, find a quiet place where you can concentrate without being disturbed. Turn off all electronic devices because they will divert your attention from learning.

Here are a few more details on how you can motivate yourself. First, you can use "self-consequating," which involves providing consequences for your behavior.[70] These are extrinsic reinforcements or punishments, such as "after I do this assignment I will have a cup of tea" or "if I don't finish the paper this afternoon, I can't go to the movie tonight."[71] Self-praise upon completing a task is another example of self-consequating.[72] A second type of controlling motivation is "goal-oriented self-talk"; "students using goal-oriented self-talk think about or make salient various reasons they have for persisting or completing a task."[73] This type can relate to learning goals, performance goals, or task goals.[74] For example, a goal for self-talk might be learning how to play the Mozart clarinet concerto or getting a good grade for finishing an assignment. A third method is "interest enhancement," in which "students [] use strategies designed to increase their immediate enjoyment or the situational interest they experience while completing an activity," particularly with boring or repetitive tasks.[75] An example of interest enhancement is making studying a game.[76] Finally, students can use "environmental structuring," which is reducing distractions or increasing readiness for studying by changing location or avoiding activities like eating and drinking.[77] Other examples of environmental structuring include keeping a schedule calendar or allocating specific times each day to studying.[78]

Students can also affect their motivation by regulating their emotions so that they can exert the effort to complete a task.[79] It is especially important for students to control negative emotions, such as negative self-talk and test anxiety, because they can affect outcome and self-efficacy expectations.[80] One strategy to overcome negative emotions is self-talk, such as "You are not going to compare yourself to your classmates" or "You worry too much; You are progressing in finishing this task."[81]

Finally, the most important factor is to take charge of your learning. When you are in charge of your learning, you will be motivated.

Exercises: Motivation

1. Think about a paper you had difficulty writing in high school or college? Would writing the paper have been easier if you had been more motivated? How could you have motivated yourself to write that paper better?
2. Do you set goals when you do a task? Do you see how setting goals can help you do better? Think about a class you did not do well in in high school or college? What goals could you have set for that class?
3. Did you set learning goals in high school? Can you see why they are more effective for motivation than other types of goals? Think about a paper you did poorly on in high school or college, and how learning goals could have helped you with that paper.
4. Do students who learn for learning's sake do better than other students in college?
5. Think about a class you did well in in high school; What was the subjective value of that course for you?

6. Think about how a class you took in high school or college helped you in a later class? Can you see the importance of long-term goals?
7. What are your long-term goals for law practice or business? Are you accomplishing them?
8. When you undertake a task, do you consider whether your approach will help you achieve your goal?
9. When you undertake a task, do you consider how well you can do that task?
10. Do you draw on past successes to help you set efficacy expectations for the future?
11. Did you think about your learning environment when you were in college? Were there any ways you could have improved your learning environment in college?
12. Have you ever used emotional motivators? Think of a class you could have done better in if you had used emotional motivators?
13. When you learn something, do you view it as a task or as something new you can learn (novelty)? Can you see how adopting a novel approach could help your learning?
14. Think about a hard project you want to do. Think how you can create the expectancy of creating that project?
15. Do you use self-consequating? What self-consequating things do you think will be successful for you?
16. How can you use interest enhancement to help motivate you?
17. Do you try to reduce distractions while learning?
18. Do you have negative emotions about learning? How can you reduce these negative emotions?
19. Do you take charge of your learning, or do you expect others to take charge of your learning? Are you an active or passive learner?
20. Create a mission statement for your life, for your cross-cultural learning.

IV. Discovering Differences Among Cultures

Those who deal with individuals from other cultures must be able to communicate with those individuals. As one author has declared, "Inaccurate attributions can cause lawyers to make significant errors in their representation

Developing Cross-Cultural Competence

of clients."[82] It can also cause a business person to blow an important deal. This section will discuss how to learn about other cultures.

A definition of culture that works well with cross-cultural competence is "A culture is a socially transmitted or socially constructed constellation consisting of such things as practices, competencies, ideas, schemas, symbols, values, norms, institutions, goals, constitutive rules, artifacts, and modifications of the physical environment."[83] A person can be a member of more than one culture.[84]

The predominant view today is that "basic human characteristics are common to all members of the species . . . and that culture influences the development and display of them."[85] In other words, genetics creates the basics; culture the details. For instance, "Both Jews and Japanese may attach importance to being good members of the community, broadly speaking. But Jews may demonstrate being good members of the community by participating in public prayer whereas Japanese may do so by suppressing self-expression to promote group harmony."[86]

The foundation for developing cross-cultural competence is knowing the other culture. Here are some examples:

Differences in the language spoken is often a difficult barrier between people from different countries. Even when individuals from different countries speak the same language, there can be variations in sarcasm, idioms, accents, dialects, voice inflections, colloquialisms, slang, and abbreviations.[87] (If you watch British television or foreign movies you can easily see these differences.)

A major difference among cultures is individualistic versus collectivistic societies. Collectivistic societies include Japan, China, India and Pakistan, while Western societies tend to be individualistic.[88] One author has noted,

> In an individualistic culture, people are socialized to have individual goals and are praised for achieving these goals. They are encouraged to make their own plans and "do their own thing." Individualists need to assert themselves and do not find competition threatening. By contrast, in a collective

culture, people are socialized to think in terms of the group, to work for the betterment of the group, and to integrate individual and group goals. Collectivists use group membership to predict behavior. Because collectivists are accepted for who they are and accordingly feel less need to talk, silence plays a more important role in their communication style.[89]

Signs for credibility can vary among cultures.[90] What you think might satisfy credibility may not satisfy a person from another country. Similarly, different societies have different ways of indicating status.[91]

Be aware of differences in body language and facial expressions, making sure that you are reading these in relation to the other person's culture, instead of yours. For example, a firm handshake is part of Western culture.[92] On the other hand, many places in Asia consider a handshake aggressive and prefer to bow. In parts of Africa, a limp handshake is employed, instead of a firm one.

Be careful with hand gestures. For example, "the 'OK' sign in Greece, Spain or Brazil means you are calling someone an a**hole. In Turkey, it's meant to be an insult towards gay people."[93]

Eye contact in Western cultures is a sign of confidence and attentiveness.[94] However, in many Asian, African, and Latin American countries, unbroken eye contact is regarded as aggressive and confrontational.

Tone of voice can also be an issue. Some cultures use a high-pitched voice during conversation, which can be confusing to those who come from other cultures.[95]

Even sitting positions vary by culture.[96] For example, sitting cross-legged is disrespectful in Japan. Similarly, personal space can be different between countries.[97]

90% of facial expressions have universal meanings. These include expressions for happiness, sadness, surprise, fear, disgust, and anger.[98] However, people from different cultures may vary in their perceptions of universal emotions.[99] In addition, "regions varied in how frequently different facial expressions were produced as a function of which contexts were most salient."[100]

Developing Cross-Cultural Competence
25

All aspects of cross-cultural competence are important to effectively interact with others. For example, three psychologists have emphasized religion as an important component of cross-cultural competency.[101] They asserted that "religion should be fully integrated into cross-cultural research for four reasons: (a) religion, by itself, occupies a substantial role in people's lives across different cultures; (b) religion has been found to be a strong predictor of important life domains among individuals all over the world; (c) religion has a strong influence on cross-cultural dimensions; and (d) culture also influences and shapes religious beliefs and practices."[102] For instance, differences in the manifestation of religious faith contribute to the divergence of Egyptian and Iranian cultures.[103]

Here are some etiquette guides for international travelers and business people:

Japan: https://www.lonelyplanet.com/articles/japan-dos-and-donts
Thailand: https://www.tripsavvy.com/thailand-etiquette-dos-and-donts-1458305
China: https://www.travelchinaguide.com/essential/etiquette.htm
Saudi Arabia: https://www.commisceo-global.com/resources/country-guides/saudi-arabia-guide
India: http://www.ediplomat.com/np/cultural_etiquette/ce_in.htm
Great Britain: https://studylinks.com/british-etiquette-a-guide-for-international-students

Exercise: Learning about Other Cultures

Using one of the above cultural guides (or one for another country if you prefer), compare that nation's culture to your own. What are the differences and similarities between the cultures? Reflect on how you would deal with the differences if you had to go to the other country to negotiate a contract. Think how you would adjust if you had to live in that foreign country for several months or years. Consider how you would treat foreign business visitors to your local office.

There are often regional cultural differences within countries. For example, "Cultures that subsist by herding typically attach more importance to honor and reputation than do people from agrarian societies. If a person in a herding culture develops a reputation as someone who vociferously defends threats against his honor, his livelihood is less likely to be taken away by rustlers."[104] This can have long-lasting effects: "Whites in the southern United States derive historically from Scotch-Irish herding societies, but Whites in the North are more likely to be descended from farmers. Therefore, D. Cohen and colleagues proposed that values about honor and reputation are more likely to be present in Southerners and that Southerners are more likely to respond to insults with violence."[105]

These regional differences create other cultural differences. "Collectivism was highest in the Deep South, and individualism was highest in the Mountain West and Great Plains. Hawaii was found to be especially collectivist, perhaps because of the high proportion of people of Asian descent living in Hawaii. . . . Poverty and population density were associated with greater collectivism. . . . Finally, . . . minorities were generally more collectivist."[106]

Differences in socio-economic status and social class also create differences among cultures. Because "[t]hose of high socioeconomic status are more able to control their environments and influence others, ... the culture of high socioeconomic status values control and agency, whereas the culture of low socioeconomic status more highly values flexibility, integrity, and resilience."[107] For example, "rock music emphasizes self-actualization, going against the grain, and making the world accommodate and conform. Country music is more likely to emphasize adapting to challenges and maintaining integrity and resiliency."[108]

Socio-economic factors can also produce variation within characteristics, such as individualism. "In lower class South Rockaway [NYC], individualism focuses on self-sufficiency and self-determination and on surviving in a bad system. In relatively upperclass Beach Channel, individualism is about personal success and achievement, and success is linked to hard work, tenacity, and self-confidence. In upper class Carter Hill, the focus is on appreciating children's uniqueness and individuality, cultivating their success and happiness, and encouraging them to feel they can do anything."[109]

There is a great deal of cultural diversity in the United States. People have come to this land from many different nations at many different times. All the world's races and ethnicities exist in this country. We have a multitude of religions, and many people are agnostic or atheist. Political views extend from the far right to the far left. Our country is a land of riches, but there is great poverty in both rural and urban areas. Individuals have wide-ranging interests in recreation, music, art, and everything else that makes for a good life. They have differing values, beliefs, and biases.

There have been several papers on cross-culture competence for doctors. For example, one study noted, "The role of mistrust is one important aspect in the African American experience of medical care. African American history in the United States includes a protracted period of slavery, post-Emancipation 'Jim Crow' discrimination and persecution in the South, and an extended period of socioeconomic disadvantages during ghettoization in northern cities."[110] More specifically, "there was the Tuskegee syphilis study in which informed consent was not used and indicated treatment was withheld without the patients' knowledge."[111]

Understanding a group's religion is also important in health care. The same Report observed that "Many African Americans have either a religious orientation or a viewpoint grounded in African American social and cultural history, which may emphasize a holistic approach to health and healthcare. Religion is a source of enormous emotional support for African Americans, and religious observance or religiosity can, in many regards, correlate with improved health outcomes."[112] Similarly, Islam has become the religion of many African-Americans, which affects how they view and deal with medical professionals.

The race of the physician can also affect how Blacks view health care. "[O]nly 22% of respondents expressed a preference for an African-American physician, but those who did were more likely to express satisfaction with a racially concordant physician. The Commonwealth Fund's HealthCare Quality Survey found that African Americans were more likely to rate their physicians as excellent if the physician was also African American. Racially discordant clinical dyads were found to be less likely to engage in a participatory communication process."[113]

Finally, one must be careful not to think that since a person is a member of a culture (or cultures) that they don't exhibit differences, perhaps even significant differences, from other members of that culture. As one writer has stated, "A broad definition of culture recognizes that no two people can have exactly the same experiences and thus no two people will interpret or predict in precisely the same ways. Culture is enough of an abstraction that people can be part of the same culture, yet make different decisions in the particular. People can also reject norms and values from their culture."[114] In addition, "Culture is dynamic and the importance of different identities change as the situation changes."[115]

Exercises: Other Cultures

1. Identify assumptions you made about individuals from other cultures that were wrong.
2. Do you have difficulty dealing with people from a particular cultural group? Try to figure out why this is so.
3. Do you have difficulty dealing with people from other generations? Try to figure out why this is so. (Age is a part of culture.)

V. Cross-Cultural Competence for Lawyers and Business Professionals

Best Practices for Legal Education, a key study on legal education, stressed the importance of developing "the capacity to deal sensitively and effectively with clients, colleagues and others from a range of social, economic and ethnic backgrounds, identifying and responding positively and appropriately to issues of culture and disability that might affect communication techniques and influence a client's objectives."[116] It added, "Cross-cultural competence is a skill that can be taught."[117]

Two scholars declared, "We believe that all lawyering is cross-cultural, so teaching about cross-cultural lawyering is necessary if clinical students are to provide quality representation to their clients. We also believe that the measure of good cross-cultural lawyering is the respect a lawyer has for her client's dignity, voice, and story, and the lawyer's understanding of her own biases and ethnocentric world views."[118]

Cultural competence is also vital for business people. As one writer declared:

> We know that in most organizations today, you can't get a promotion to the C-suite and you're probably not going to move up to leadership level without some kind of international experience or international assignment. Organizations are looking for people who have either international experience prior to coming to the company or who are willing to go on to an international assignment to develop this cultural com-petency.[119]

A. Developing Cross-Cultural Competency for Lawyers and Business People: Mindset and Awareness

Legal culture is a culture, and it encompasses many microcultures.[120] The same is true for businesses.

In general, "When lawyers and clients come from different cultures, several aspects of the attorney-client interaction may be implicated. The capacity to form trusting relationships, to evaluate credibility, to develop client-centered case strategies and solutions, to gather information and to attribute the intended meaning from behavior and expressions are all affected by cultural experiences."[121] Also, don't forget that your client or a business associate may come from a culture with a different legal system than yours (civil v. common law).

Developing A Cross-Cultural Mindset

The first step in developing cross-cultural competence is to develop a cross-cultural mindset or commitment. Self-regulated students, lawyers, and business professionals develop attitudes and habits. The first attitude I want you to develop is "I will always consider the other person or persons–clients, judges, opposing attorneys, staff, business partners–in a professional interaction." The second attitude relates to the first one: "I will always consider the other person's or persons' cultural background, and I will strive to treat that person or persons appropriately within their cultural background." Habits that will help you with this attitude include 1) I will always consider the other persons in my business and social interactions, 2) I will listen carefully to the people I interact with, 3) I will be sensitive to what others are thinking and feeling, 4) I will respect other persons' cultures. 5) I will try to make people from other cultures feel comfortable, etc.

Exercise: Cross-Cultural Competence Mindset

1. Reflect on the attitude you have held to people from other cultures in the past (both foreign and from your country). Did you think about their culture at all? Did you think your culture was superior to theirs? Did you make fun of their culture?
2. How did your attitudes to other cultures help or hurt you in your legal, business or social interactions? Think how being culturally sensitive could help you in your career? (Think about your specific profession.)

Completely finish the above exercises before you look at the comment below.

Comment

Developing a cross-cultural competence mindset is the first and most important step in becoming cross-culturally competent. Developing cross-cultural competence may be a lot of work, but the work you put in will be worth it. First, you will open up countless job opportunities. Second, you should advance more easily in your career. (As I have noted before, most jobs in your country will require cross-cultural skills.) Three, it will make your life easier because of fewer uncomfortable interactions.

Developing Awareness of Cross-Cultural Situations

The second step in developing cross-cultural competence is awareness–the ability to recognize situations that involve cultural differences. Awareness is a key part of a cross-cultural mindset. Recognize that other people may have a cultural background that is very different from yours. (Part of awareness is understanding your culture, including its weaknesses.) Then, develop the habit of trying to understand those differences. This will not be easy, but I have included exercises in this book to help you begin the process. Then, practice, practice, practice.

The first step in developing cross-cultural awareness is being aware of other people in general.

Exercises: Awareness of Other People

1. Do you notice how other people are feeling? Family? Friends? Business associates? Clients? Your secretary? Employees? Waiters? Store clerks? Do you notice when someone is ill? Do you notice when someone is upset?
2. Do you consider the effects your actions will have on other people? All the time? Sometimes? Rarely? Never?
3. Do you notice when business associates do something insensitive or unethical?
4. Think about situations in your job that require awareness of the feelings of others. In your family. In your social interactions?
5. You are seated on a subway or a bus. Do you notice when a person who is standing needs to sit down because of age or disability?

The best way to develop awareness of others is to look around and reflect. Don't bury your head in the sand all the time. Notice that a fellow employee is having a bad day. Try to figure out why your boss is in a bad mood. Be aware that your waiter is swamped, and it may take a little longer for your food to come out.

Once you have developed awareness of others, you can start to develop cross-cultural awareness. Traditional client-centered views of lawyering saw clients as being like lawyers except for their educational levels and knowledge of the law.[122] However, anyone who has practiced law knows there are many, many differences between lawyers and most clients. A lawyer ethnocentric (one-size-fits-all) model can weaken the attorney-client relationship.[123] For example,

> Jacobs reminds us that clients labeled difficult by textbooks espousing client-centered lawyering might be resisting the lawyer's invitation to participate in the lawyering process. Rather than dismiss the client as difficult, lawyers need to ask ourselves why the client might be resisting our invitation. Might the client's response be a reaction to behavior by the lawyer who fails to recognize "the real client in her full context – culturally, politically and economically?" Or based on the client's perception of a lawyer who is culturally different from her?[124]

One author has suggested that to overcome these kinds of problems, a lawyer should "develop[ ] awareness and knowledge of one's own culture; develop[ ] awareness of the client's culture; and learn[ ] specific skills to minimize the impact of one's own biases and prejudices toward the multicultural interaction."[125] These are the precise skills I am asking you to work on throughout this guide.

The areas where cultural differences are most likely to occur for a lawyer or business person are 1) proxemics ("perception and use of personal and interpersonal space"), 2) kinesics ("way in which bodily movements are used and interpreted;"), 3) time and priority considerations, 4) narrative preferences (chronological storytelling versus narrative storytelling), 5) relational perspectives ("individual vs. collective orientations"), 6) and scientific orientation.[126] For example, concerning proxemics, "Many cultures, including Latin American, African, Black American, Indonesian, Arab, South American, and French, prefer discourse at a much closer distance than White

American culture finds comfortable or appropriate. Other cultures, such as the British, maintain a greater distance than traditional American custom."[127]

Exercise: Cross-Cultural Awareness

1. Are you generally aware of cultural differences between you and another person, or do you ignore them?

Exercises: Developing Cross-Cultural Awareness

1. Think about your practice or business. What are the cultures that your clients or customers come from? What do you know about their cultures?
2. Start with the culture that constitutes the largest group in your business from another culture. What do you know about the cultures of people from this group? What do you need to know about this culture in relation to your practice or business? (Obviously, it is impossible to know everything about a culture.)

Try the above with both foreign cultures and cultures within your country.

Also, be aware that an individual is probably a member of more than one culture. Similarly, be aware that people do not always adopt the characteristics of their culture. Sometimes they reject the culture they grew up in or currently live in. (Ex. Someone who grew about in a highly-religious culture may reject that culture and become a person with significantly different habits, values, customs, and desires.)

Similarly, a clinical professor relates, "a student who had a Central American woman client seeking a divorce worried that the client might not feel entitled to any marital property because the student had heard that Latina women generally had a different conception of marital property than the one espoused by Massachusetts divorce law. The student therefore planned a counseling session to educate the client about Massachusetts law and empower her to ask for her legal entitlement. I encouraged the student not to assume that the client held this belief but to inquire directly of the client before she launched her planned counseling. The student did inquire of the client, and the client indicated a very strong sense of entitlement to marital property, including payment of debt."[128]

Exercises: Individuals from Multiple Cultures

1. Are you from multiple cultures? How has this affected you?
2. Think of individuals you know well that are from multiple cultures. What cultures are they from? What characteristics does the individual from multiple culture exhibit? How has this affected them? How has this affected how you deal with them/
3. Have you rejected the culture you grew up in (in whole or in part)? How is this affected you?
4. Do you know anyone who has rejected the culture they grew up in? How has this affected them?

Next, try to appreciate the foreign culture. Other cultures are fascinating if you look at them in the right way. What do you like about that culture? Their music? Their food? Their art? Their manners? Their business practices? If you find things you like about culture, you will be better able to deal with other aspects of the culture. In other words, be curious.

Exercise: Appreciating Other Cultures

1. Picture a foreign culture you are interested in? What do you find in that culture that interests you? Can you find other things in that culture that are interesting? (I love French food. Okay, maybe I should take a trip to France. French is an interesting language. Maybe I should learn it. What is French music like?)
2. Do the same thing with another culture from your country.

B. Some General Techniques for Overcoming Cross-Cultural Problems

Of course, you must not only be aware of cultural differences; you must be able to deal with them effectively. A key component of this is patience. Don't show frustration when someone from another culture says or does something that seems strange to you. Patience and cultural humility especially helps when you were not aware of the cultural difference.

Developing Interpersonal Rapport

Develop interpersonal rapport with people from other cultures. A lawyer should listen to their clients' stories with empathy.[129] A business person should do the same with their customers or business partners. "Empathy is the capacity to understand or feel what another person is experiencing from within the other being's frame of reference, i.e., the capacity to place oneself in another's position. Empathy is seeing with another's eyes, listening with another's ears, and feelings with another's heart of another."[130] In other words, put yourself in the other person's shoes. An important part of this "involves imagining their perspective in an unbiased and neutral manner."[131]

I grew up in a part of the South that was very conservative. I didn't know any openly gay men growing up. I majored in music in college. There are many gay men in music. I got to know these men, understand them, and accept them. Today, some of my closest friends are gay.

Exercise: Developing Interpersonal Rapport with People from other Cultures

1. Think about a friend from a different culture. How did you develop a friendship with this person? When you first learned they were different how did you react? Were you bothered by the differences? How did you overcome the differences?
2. Do you have multiple friendships with individuals from foreign cultures? Why or why not?
3. Do you have empathy with other people? Do you think other people would agree that you have empathy? How do you express empathy for others? Is

your empathy limited to your friends and family, or do you have empathy for your clients and business associates, too?
4. Can you put yourself in the shoes of others?

Critical Listening

Effective communication is essential in cross-cultural competence, and, therefore, a lawyer (or business professional) must be an active and critical listener. As one author has written, "Active listening requires that an attorney listen carefully to his client's story and respond in a way that makes the client feel that he has been understood. As a result a client is less likely to omit important facts or view the lawyer as a hostile interrogator."[132] Similarly, "By focusing on the client, the lawyer can gather culture-sensitive information and use that information to ensure respect for the client's culture and wishes."[133]

Adopt the attitude that you will be an active listener rather than a passive one. Put yourself in your listener's shoes. Context is a key to critical listening so try to determine the context. Listen underneath your client's story. When listening to a client, you should realize that the client is not a lawyer, and the client may not present the case in the most comprehensible manner. It is your job to ask questions so that you are clear on what the client wants you to do.

A critical listener is non-judgmental (suspension of judgement).[134] A lawyer is there to help clients, not judge them.

Other techniques that can help you deal with cross-cultural problems include reflection, evaluation, self-monitoring,

Reflection

Developing cross-cultural competence requires reflection. Reflect on yourself. Reflect about others. Reflect about other cultures and their attributes. Reflect on how to deal with individuals from other cultures.

Reflection is "an active thought process aimed at understanding and subsequent improvement."[135] Furthermore, "reflection facilitates [thinkers] to draw from their previous practic[al] experience and to apply that which is relevant to new and unfamiliar [] situations."[136]

Being a reflective thinker starts at the metacognitive level. Metacognition involves "knowledge about one's own knowledge and knowledge about one's own performance."[137] It allows "learners to understand and monitor their cognitive processes."[138] "Metacognition involves the understanding of how a task is performed."[139] Stated differently, ""Metacognition refers to awareness of one's own knowledge—what one does and doesn't know—and one's ability to understand, control, and manipulate one's cognitive processes. It includes knowing when and where to use particular strategies for learning and problem solving as well as how and why to use specific strategies. Metacognition is the ability to use prior knowledge to plan a strategy for approaching a learning task, take necessary steps to problem solve, reflect on and evaluate results, and modify one's approach as needed."[140] In sum, metacognition is one's inner voice or inner critic, and a self-regulated thinker develops her inner voice.

Your inner voice asks you questions about what you are doing. It asks you to relate what you are doing to what you have done previously. It asks you to criticize what you are doing or have done (self-monitoring and evaluation). It asks you about the implications and consequences of what you doing. It also makes you think about alternative actions.

One way to become a reflective learner is to keep a journal and write in it every night.

Evaluation (Learning from Your Mistakes)

Part of cross-cultural competence is the ability to learn from your mistakes. Do you think about what went wrong when you have made a cross-cultural error?

With evaluation, you consider how well your cross-cultural competence process worked. Did I handle the situation properly? What have

I learned to improve my processes in the future? (Do this with every cross-cultural interaction.)

Self-Monitoring

Self-monitoring is a type of evaluation that occurs while you are reading, learning, or doing. It is concentrating on how well you are doing a process while you are doing it. It helps you avoid mistakes, and it also helps you slow down your thinking so that you are less likely to make a mistake. With cross-cultural competence, you should be self-monitoring for snap judgments, mistakes, cognitive biases, and stereotypical thinking.

Questions: Reflection, Evaluation, and Self-Monitoring

Answer these questions using reflection, evaluation, and self-monitoring.

1. You have business visitors from Saudi Arabia coming to your office next week to negotiate a contract. Think about the kinds of things you need to do to prepare for their visit. They are Muslims. Brainstorm.[141]
2. You have business visitors from India. Your boss has asked you to take them out to dinner. You know of a terrific Indian restaurant. Do you take your visitors to that restaurant?
3. You are a mediator in a legal dispute. One of the parties is a poor black woman and the other party is a well-educated Chinese-American man. How would you handle this situation?
4. You are a mediator in a legal dispute. You are a middle-class Latino women. One of the parties is a middle-class Latino woman and the other one is a White man. What do you do?
5. You have business visitors from Saudi Arabia. You plan to take them to your favorite bar for a good time. Is this a good idea?
6. You are starting a job at a legal clinic. Most of your clients are poor, and many are immigrants. How do you prepare to meet with your clients?

Comments

1. I would first do some research on Saudi Arabian culture. Do they have any business customs that are different from your country's? What types of expressions and body language should you avoid. Should you use humor or avoid it? If you are taking them out for a meal, do they have any dietary practices that are different than yours? How will this affect what restaurant you choose? If you are taking them out for an evening entertainment, what entertainment would be proper? Anything else?
2. To avoid embarrassment, ask them what type of restaurant your visitors would like to go to.
3. The main thing you need to do is to consider both parties' cultures. A mediator must treat all parties fairly and objectively. To do this, the mediator must respect all parties' cultures. Repeat this problem with the parties coming from different cultures.
4. This type of problem arises all the time for mediators and judges. Mediators and judges must be impartial regardless of who appears before them. Hopefully, the section on cognitive biases below will help you avoid any potential problems.
5. Most people from Saudi Arabia are Muslims, and Muslims generally do not drink.
6. First, and foremost, be patient. Second, be empathetic and nonjudgmental. Clients want to feel that you care. Similarly, remember that what is wrong in your culture may not be in theirs. Next, explain carefully and make sure the client understands. However, never, never talk down to your client. Everyone deserves respect. Also, remember that your client is probably nervous. Finally, let your client know that you are there for them, and tell them how they can get in touch with you.

C. Thinking Critically to Overcome Cross-Cultural Problems

Dilbert Cartoon: Scott Adams

Dogbert is sitting on a park bench talking to a man.

Panel One. Man: "I teach my kids that these things are right and these things are wrong. Period. End of Story."
Panel Two. Dogbert: "Wouldn't that teach them to believe anything they're told without applying any critical thought?"
Panel Three. Man: "I don't think about that." Dogbert: "Duh."

    Using critical thinking skills will help you develop cross-cultural competence.[142] You must practice to develop critical thinking skills (create habits).[143]
    Critical thinking is "[t]he intellectually disciplined process of actively and skillfully conceptualizing, applying, analyzing, synthesizing, and/or evaluating information gathered from, or generated by, observation, experience, reflection, reasoning, or communication, as a guide to belief and action."[144] "It is . . . automatically questioning if the information presented is factual, reliable, evidence-based, and unbiased."[145] It is "a collection of thinking skills [thinking processes] that advance intellectual focus, motivation, and engagement with new ideas."[146] Critical thinking supplies the thought process for evaluating arguments, and the ability to reject faulty ones.[147]
    Critical thinking involves a rigorous approach to reasoning, making judgments and decisions, and problem solving. It "avoids common pitfalls, such as seeing only one side of an issue, discounting new evidence that disconfirms your ideas, reasoning from passion rather than logic, failing to support statements with evidence, and so on."[148]

1. It is metacognitive and reflective.
2. It is evaluative.
3. It is skeptical and moderately distrusting.
4. It is analytic.
5. It tries to be unbiased and open-minded.
6. It is effortful, potentially time-consuming, and mentally taxing.[149]

<u>Questioning Authority</u>

A critical thinker questions authority–both people and texts. Do not uncritically rely on an expert. Ask hard questions. Why is this person considered an expert in her field? What is her education, experience, and other credentials? How is she viewed in her field? Is she a careful researcher/scholar? Does she use critical thinking in her work? Consult other experts on an issue to make sure you have all views. Use your critical skills when evaluating an expert's work.

Reflections: Questioning Authority

1. When you read or hear experts, do you automatically accept what they write or say as true or correct?
2. When you were in school, did you automatically accept what your teachers told you?
3. How do you question authority?

Assumptions and Evidence

A critical thinker recognizes assumptions (and opinions) and does not treat them like facts. An assumption is "a willingness to accept something as true without question or proof."[150] It is taking something for granted. Facts are supported by evidence. Building an argument on assumptions is like building a house with no foundation.

Essential to critical thinking is the ability to support one's ideas and conclusions with evidence, rather than relying on assumptions.[151] Effective thinkers must be able to distinguish between conclusions and supporting evidence.[152] However, many people lack a clear grasp of what constitutes evidence.[153] Students' inability to support a conclusion should tell them that their conclusion may be faulty. In addition, critical thinking requires looking at all the evidence, even evidence that doesn't support your conclusion. I will discuss this topic more below under the Semmelweis effect.

Reflections: Assumptions and Evidence

1. Can you recognize whether a statement or conclusion is based on evidence or on assumptions?
2. When you read or hear a statement, do you try to determine whether that statement is based on an assumption?
3. Do you make sure that your arguments are based on facts and evidence? Do you consider evidence that both supports and undermines your arguments?

Exercises: Assumptions

Are these assumptions or facts.

1. The teacher doesn't like me because I am Martian.
2. Cigarette smoking is dangerous for your health.
3. We must examine your childhood to determine why you fear snakes.
4. The assault was a hate crime.
5. Students have different learning styles.
6. He is the murderer; I saw him shoot the deceased.
7. This crime could have been prevented if we had stronger gun laws.
8. This massacre would never have happened if church goers were allowed to carry guns in our state.
9. There is no correlation between a state's gun control laws and its homicide rate.
10. Read *Plessy v. Ferguson*, 165 U.S. 537 (1896). What assumptions support the reasoning in this case? Evaluate the assumptions. Focus on the Fourteenth Amendment analysis.

Comments

1. Assumption. Maybe, but aren't there lots of other reasons a teacher may not like a student. For example, the student may not be hard working. In addition, the student may be misinterpreting the teacher. Maybe she treats all students the same way.
2. Fact. There is scientific proof supporting this.

3. Assumption. Maybe something that happened in your childhood caused your fear of snakes, but there might be other reasons.
4. This is an assumption until someone offers evidence of a hate crime.
5. This is a commonly held neuromyth. Researchers have proven that students do not exhibit learning styles, like visual learners versus auditory learners.
6. Still an assumption. The police would have to prove that the shooter caused the death. Maybe, he was also poisoned. Also, it might have been self-defense.
7. There is no proof of causation here.
8. Same answer.
9. Fact. Did I catch you? There is a study backing up the above statement.[154] Of course, a true critical thinker would have also looked for contrary studies.
10. A. That "separate, but equal" truly is equal. B. What do you think of this statement: "The object of the amendment was undoubtedly to enforce the absolute equality of the two races before the law, but, in the nature of things, it could not have been intended to abolish distinctions based upon color, or to enforce social, as distinguished from political, equality, or a commingling of the two races upon terms unsatisfactory to either. Laws permitting, and even requiring, their separation in places where they are liable to be brought into contact do not necessarily imply the inferiority of either race to the other, and have been generally, if not universally, recognized as within the competency of the state legislatures in the exercise of their police power." Start with the Fourteenth Amendment "could not have been intended to abolish distinctions based upon color. . ." Is this a fair assumption? What was the Fourteenth Amendment intended to do? Other questions: Can the social be separated from the political? This case assumes it can be. Can you have equality without social equality? The Court assumes there can be. Was commingling unsatisfactory to both races? The Court seems to think it is. If it is, why were there so many cases on this topic? Do satisfied people sue? "Laws permitting, and even requiring, their separation in places where they are liable to be brought into contact do not necessarily imply the inferiority of either race to the other. . ." Is this a fact or an assumption? Since the Court gives it no support, it must be an assumption. Do you think the assumption is correct?

How does Justice Harlan's dissent attack the above assumptions. Which opinion is more convincing?
Plessy is an excellent example of how bad assumptions can be used to support a bad decision. Today, we can see all the problems with the case's reasoning. Yet, the decision stood for over 50 years.

Developing and Evaluating Alternatives

Developing and evaluating alternatives is also an important critical thinking skill. Beginners usually stop with the first possibility; experts try to think up all reasonable possibilities because the first one may not be the best one. Experts reflect; they look at problems from different angles (reframe the problem); they turn things over in their minds.[155]

Reflections: Developing and Evaluating Alternatives

1. When you are writing an argument or making a conclusion, do you consider all reasonable alternatives, or do you stop with the first idea you come up with?
2. Are you critical of all the alternatives?
3. Come up with all the arguments for and against gun control. Carefully criticize everything you came up with, even arguments you support.

Flawed Reasoning

Critical thinking also requires "the ability to recognize flawed reasoning or flawed arguments derived from claims."[156] With deductive thinking, the conclusion follows from true premises, so the key is to test the premises.[157] However, other types of reasoning, such as analytical reasoning and inductive reasoning, involve a degree of uncertainty.[158] Thus, critical thinking often involves judging of the degree of uncertainty.

Reflections: Flawed Reasoning

1. Do you look for flawed reasoning in your arguments and conclusions?

2. Do you look for flawed reasoning in the arguments and conclusions of others?
3. Can you recognize a deductive argument? An inductive argument? Reasoning by analogy? How do you deal well with uncertainty?

Making Inferences

Drawing inferences is a key thinking process. "An inference is an idea or conclusion that's drawn from evidence and reasoning. An inference is an educated guess."[159] It is "the process of inferring things based on what is already known."[160]

One writer has asserted, "the willingness and ability to see that what we believe may be false, and in such cases, to see what would count as evidence against our belief. . ." is important for evaluating inferences.[161] Consequently, "the fundamental skill to be acquired by a critical thinker is the ability to recognize inferential connections holding between statements, where this would include the ability to understand the possibility that what we believe might be false and the ability to identify the sorts of evidence that would undermine our beliefs."[162]

Reflections: Inferences

1. Can you recognize inferences?
2. Can you ascertain whether an inference is valid?

Exercises: Inferences

What inferences can you draw from the below.

1. You are at a baseball game with a friend. Suddenly, you smell cigar smoke. Your friend makes a face.
2. The murder victim was hit violently several times with a hammer.
3. The watch dog didn't bark when the burglar broke into the house.

4. You are driving on a highway. You see the driver in front of you look to his left.
5. The suspect ran when the police approached him.

Comments

1. Your friend doesn't like cigars.
2. It was a crime of passion.
3. The dog knew the burglar (The Hound of the Baskervilles)
4. He is going to move into the left lane.
5. The suspect was guilty.

You need to critically test the inference to make sure it is reasonable. There are two types of inferences: 1) deductive inferences–if the premise is true the conclusion must be true and 2) inductive inferences–"requires weighing evidence and judging probability, not proof."[163] With deductive inferences, you just need to test to see whether the premise is true, but inductive premises require a closer look. "An impermissible inference . . . occurs when the reasoner concludes based on scant evidence."[164] Faulty inferences often create stereotypes.

Exercises: Inferences

Criticize the following inferences.

1. He doesn't have an alibi for the time of the murder. He must be the murderer.
2. At an airport, you see a man running for a gate. You infer that he is anxious to meet a friend. (This is before only passengers were allowed in the boarding area.)
3. The Supreme Court denied cert. One can conclude that the Supreme Court agreed with the lower court.

Comments

1. People are alone for lots of reasons. Being alone, by itself, does not prove someone is guilty.
2. He might also be late for his plane.
3. I hope you lawyers got this one. The Supreme Court accepts only a few cases a year. Denying cert. doesn't suggest anything.

The morale of this story is to not make inferences uncritically.

Critical Thinking Checklist

1. Evaluate authority.
2. Look for and evaluate assumptions.
3. Support ideas and conclusions with evidence.
4. Look for evidence (or lack of evidence) in others' arguments.
5. Look for and evaluate alternatives.
6. Look for flawed reasoning and flawed arguments.
7. Test inferences.
8. Use reflection, self-monitoring, and evaluation.
9. Keep an open mind. Avoid cognitive biases (see below).

D. Cross-Cultural Competence and Cognitive Biases

Understanding cognitive biases is a significant part of cross-cultural competence.[165] Lawyers and business professionals must be able to recognize both their biases and the biases of others to be competent lawyers and business professionals and deal with people from other cultures.

Cognitive biases (also called thinking or brain biases) are "systematic error[s] in thinking that affects the decisions and judgments that people make."[166] Everyone suffers from cognitive biases to a certain extent, even people of high intelligence.[167] Biases are a failure of rationality, not intelligence.

The human thinking process is imperfect. Like the other parts of the human body, the brain evolved. Parts of our brains today are remnants of the brains our early ancestors had, brains which had developed to survive under very different conditions from today. Evolution is not history; it is what humans are today. These remnants produce cognitive biases–ways of thinking that are different from reality.

Part of cognitive biases is human's "excessive confidence in what we believe we know and our apparent inability to acknowledge the full extent of our ignorance and the uncertainty of the world we live in."[168] "This is especially true of divisive political issues. Your mind cannot master and retain sufficiently detailed knowledge about many of them. You must rely on your community. But if you are not aware that you are piggybacking on the knowledge of others, it can lead to hubris."[169] In other words, critical thinkers recognize when they lack the knowledge to be a critical thinker in a particular area or on a particular subject.

Here are some key cognitive biases to consider for cross-cultural competence:

1. Bias blind spot: "The tendency to see oneself as less biased than other people, or to be able to identify more cognitive biases in others than in oneself."
2. Confirmation bias: "The tendency to search for, interpret, focus on and remember information in a way that confirms one's preconceptions."
3. Curse of knowledge: "When better-informed people find it extremely difficult to think about problems from the perspective of lesser-informed people."
4. Empathy gap: "The tendency to underestimate the influence or strength of feelings, in either oneself or others."
5. Essentialism: "Categorizing people and things according to their essential nature, in spite of variations."
6. Framing effect: "Drawing different conclusions from the same information, depending on how that information is presented."

7. Halo effect: "The tendency for a person's positive or negative traits to 'spill over' from one personality area to another in others' perceptions of them."
8. Illusion of control: "The tendency to overestimate one's degree of influence over other external events."
9. In-group bias: "The tendency for people to give preferential treatment to others they perceive to be members of their own groups."
10. Optimism bias: "The tendency to be over-optimistic, overestimating favorable and pleasing outcomes."
11. Ostrich effect: "Ignoring an obvious (negative) situation."
12. Overconfidence effect: "Excessive confidence in one's own answers to questions."
13. Projection bias: "he tendency to unconsciously assume that others (or one's future selves) share one's current emotional states, thoughts and values."
14. Semmelweis reflex: "The tendency to reject new evidence that contradicts a paradigm."

Don't assume that you don't suffer from these biases! Everyone suffers from the bias blind spot.[170] In one study, only 1 out of 661 subjects thought they were more biased than others.[171] As Daniel Kahneman declared, "You must accept that they are true about you."[172]

Exercises: Cognitive Biases

1. You are the senior partner at your law firm. Two associates are having a dispute. Both are taking reasonable positions. You are a white male. One of the associates is a black male and the other one is a white male. What cultural biases do you have to be aware of?
2. You are the senior partner at your law firm. Two associates are having a dispute. Both are taking reasonable positions. You are a black female. The associates are a black female and an Asian-American female. What cultural biases do you need to be aware of?

3. You are the senior partner at your law firm. Two associates are having a dispute. Both are taking reasonable positions. You are a female Latino. The associates are a white male and a black male. You have previously had a problem with the work quality of the only other black male at your firm. What cultural biases do you need to be aware of?
4. Hiring committee member: "Mr. Martin was a star basketball player at our local university. I'm sure he will be a great hire at our firm." What cognitive bias is involved?
5. Senior managing partner: "I am happy to report that I have resolved the sexual harassment situation. I talked to the offending associates, and they have promised to act better in the future."
6. Male lawyer: we have achieved gender equity at our firm. We have as many female partners as male ones." Female lawyer: "we have not yet achieved gender equity at this firm. Only 25% of the partners are women." They are talking about the same firm. Why the difference?
7. Attorney: "I am very disturbed about how your company treats minorities and women, and we need to rectify this in your case." Client: "Okay, but my problem is unique."
8. Attorney to another attorney: "Our client was overreacting. We did not insult his country."
9. "The evidence shows that attorneys who were educated at law schools in the Northwest commit more ethics violations and are involved in more malpractice suits. I know that two studies have disagreed with this, but they were outliers."
10. "The other attorneys in my firm may be subject to the in-group bias, but I treat everyone fairly."
11. "All Martians are difficult."
12. "I hate all Martians. The government should send them back to Mars."
13. Attorney: "No matter how often I explain it to him, this client just won't understand how much trouble he is in."
14. "I realize that the plaintiffs feel strongly about the case, but I'm sure they will accept a small settlement. They are poor, so they won't want to wait."
15. Prosecutor: "The judge will be disgusted by the defendant's conduct. I know I am."

16. You have a client who is addicted to heroin. You ask her why she hasn't gone to a methadone clinic?
17. Juror: "This witness must be telling the truth. He is a Martian like me."
18. Man: "I support feminism more than my other male friends."
19. Business professional: "I will get the contract when I go to Vienna. I am a great negotiator."
20. Martian: "I don't have prejudices because Martians have suffered many years of discrimination."

Comments

1. The in-group bias. You have to be careful that you don't favor the white associate just because he is of your group. Also, watch for the confirmation bias and the Semmelweis reflex working in conjunction with the in-group bias.
2. The same as 1.
3. The conformation bias. You may be unconsciously looking at the black male associate in relation to the one who has done poor work.
4. The halo effect.
5. The ostrich effect. Maybe also the optimism bias, the overconfidence effect, and the confirmation bias.
6. Framing effect.
7. Projection bias.
8. Bias blind spot.
9. Semmelweis effect.
10. Bias blind spot.
11. Essentialism (stereotyping).
12. This isn't a cognitive bias. It's explicit racism.
13. Curse of knowledge.
14. Empathy gap, illusion of control.
15. Projection bias.
16. Empathy gap.
17. In-group bias.
18. Possible bias blind spot.
19. Illusion of control, overconfidence effect, optimism bias.

20. Bias blind spot. I realize that many people will not like this answer, but it is true. As noted above, everyone has bias blind spots.

Most scholars agree that we can overcome our cognitive biases.[173] The first step in overcoming a cognitive bias is to be aware they exist and how they work. An attorney must be able to spot a bias in his thinking to overcome it. Practice looking for cognitive biases in your every day life so that you develop a habit for watching for them.

Second, slow down your thinking. When you think too quickly you rely on intuition, which is unreliable, rather than judgment. Similarly, reframe your ideas. Looking at something from another point of view will help you avoid errors in your thinking. Likewise, try to view your thoughts and problems from someone else's point of view; put yourself in the other's shoes. This will help you reframe and avoid cognitive biases.

Did you desire the outcome? If so, check your reasoning for cognitive biases. Similarly, is the outcome the same as you anticipated at the beginning?

Use the techniques of critical thinking that I mentioned above, such as checking for assumptions, considering and evaluating all alternatives, weighing all evidence equally, reflection, self-monitoring, and evaluation.

Above all, acknowledge your ignorance–lack of knowledge. Nobody knows everything. There is no shame in not knowing something. The shame is in refusing to acknowledge your ignorance and, consequently, making mistakes. If you acknowledge your ignorance, you can then seek the knowledge you need to solve a problem.

In sum, "There is an obvious difference between impartially evaluating evidence in order to come to an unbiased conclusion and building a case to justify a conclusion already drawn. In the first instance, one seeks evidence on all sides of a question, evaluates it as objectively as one can, and draws the conclusion that the evidence, in the aggregate, seems to dictate. In the second, one selectively gathers, or gives undue weight to, evidence that supports one's position while neglecting to gather, or discounting, evidence that would tell against it."[174]

VI. Cross-Cultural Competence in Business

Developing Cross-Cultural Competence

In this section, I will discuss a few problems that are especially relevant to businesses. However, lawyers and law students should read it, too.

A business team must carry out the following functions effectively:

1. Leading and following.
2. Working together.
3. Assigning and managing tasks.
4. Analyzing issues.
5. Making decisions.
6. Developing and implementing plans.[175]

Communication is the key to all of these functions.[176] In particular, be careful not to use business jargon that is common in your country, but not in the foreign culture.

One expert gave the following ten tips for international business competence:

1. Conduct executive interviews with a cultural expert to evaluate your team.
2. Identify the gaps and create a strategy for developing cultural competence.
3. Develop and implement training and coaching with a true cross-cultural expert.
4. Emphasize communication and relationship building across geographic barriers.
5. Practice active listening.
6. Be sensitive to language barriers and bridge any linguistic divides.
7. Encourage sensitivity to issues like time, local customs, religious matters, and etiquette.
8. Practice effective cross-cultural team building.
9. Solicit feedback from your team as they put training to use in the workplace.
10. Conduct a review and reassessment of your team's performance and modify your training and coaching as needed.[177]

Here is a story of how the lack of cross-cultural competence turned a meeting in Mexico into a disaster:

On Doug's first trip to visit Campbell's Mexican production facilities during his tenure as the new CEO, he held a large group meeting with employees. In his earnest but brash way, he pressed them to engage in candid dialogue with him. It didn't go well. The employees were visibly uncomfortable and it was clear that they felt the forum was disrespectful. Doug later learned that the employees thought it was inappropriate to speak so openly to leadership in a group setting. He apologized to the local management and acknowledged his lack of understanding. It was an early — and humbling — lesson in the importance of cultural fluency.[178]

While business professionals should be culturally competent, they also need to rely on local business people. As one author has written, "At the same time, the person from Chicago often has to be humbled to realize that, once they get to Shanghai, they don't have all the answers. They have to rely on this local expertise."[179]

Companies must be sensitive to how advertising is perceived by other cultures.[180] For example, "A few years ago, Pepsi apologized for an absurd Mountain Dew ad directed by Tyler, the Creator that featured a battered woman picking a perpetrator, which was really a "dewed" up goat, out of a lineup of African-American men."[181] Similar, there is a legendary story, maybe true, maybe not, that Chevy had trouble selling its vehicle, Nova, in Mexico because Nova meant "no go" in Spanish.

Here are a few more examples:[182]

US supermarket giant Wallmart completely failed in its effort to break into the German market. Analysts saw the transplanting of US corporate management and retail culture onto an alien environment as the main cause for the massive failure.

Coors had its slogan, "Turn it loose," translated into Spanish, where it became "Suffer from diarrhoea."

When the US firm Gerber started selling baby food in Africa they used the same packaging as in the US, i.e. with a picture of a baby on the label. Sales flopped and they soon realized that in Africa companies typically place pictures of contents on their labels.

Similarly, a word in one language may sound like an offensive word in another. For example, "pick" in English sounds like "pikk" in Norwegian, which means part of the male anatomy. Similarly, puff in German means brothel.

This works the same from the other direction. A word in a foreign language may sound offensive in American English. For instance, the Chinese word for "that," a common filler word in this language, is pronounced as "nà ge" or "nèi ge", which some people think sounds like a racial slur in English. Since this is a common word in Chinese, a business person working in China must be prepared to hear this word frequently without being offended.

Companies that want to be successful in this country need to market to a wide-audience, and they need to realize that there are cultural differences among the components of their market. As one writer has advised, "Personal items, like clothing and food, are not enjoyed universally the same. Subtle or distinctive nuances should be factored into product development to ensure everyone in your market niche feels included in your business outreach. Promoting new products geared toward a diverse market niche may also incite an expanded customer base interest in these products."[183] In addition, marketing to a diverse audience helps small business create roots in the community.[184]

A business also needs cross-cultural competence within its workforce to function efficiently. Managers need to let their workers know that they are important to the company, regardless of their cultural background. Of course, they also need to respect differences. Furthermore, managers should be proactive about handling problems. Never let problems fester; they will only get worse.

Here is one expert's advice on creating cultural competence within a company:

1. Conduct executive interviews with a cultural expert to evaluate your team.
2. Identify the gaps and create a strategy for developing cultural competence.
3. Develop and implement training and coaching with a true cross-cultural expert.
4. Emphasize communication and relationship building across geographic barriers.
5. Practice active listening.
6. Be sensitive to language barriers and bridge any linguistic divides.
7. Encourage sensitivity to issues like time, local customs, religious matters, and etiquette.
8. Practice effective cross-cultural team building.
9. Solicit feedback from your team as they put the training to use in the workplace.
10. Conduct a review and reassessment of your team's performance and modify your training and coaching as needed.[185]

Reflection Questions: Wrap-Up for Lawyers

1. Consider how you would react if your client accuses you of not trying to understand their problem.
2. Consider how you would react if your client accuses you of not being on their side.
3. Consider how you would react if your client accuses you of not understanding their culture.
4. You are at an important dinner with foreign lawyers. One of your clients commits a major faux pas. What do you do?

5. Take an area of law you are familiar with. Think how you would translate that area of law into everyday terms.
6. You are starting a legal clinic in the inner city. Consider ways you can get clients to come to your clinic.
7. You client is convinced that he should win his lawsuit. Right is on his side. After researching the problem, you conclude that your client cannot win at trial. How do you break the news to him?
8. You are working in an inner city clinic where most of your clients are Black and Latino. All these clients are to poor too afford a lawyer. Can you treat both groups of clients the same?
9. You work in an inner-city legal clinic. A recently-arrived immigrant from Eastern Europe has consulted you about a problem with her landlord. You have never dealt with immigrants before. How do you prepare for the initial meeting.
10. Is dealing with criminal clients different from dealing with civil ones? What extra or different steps would you take with a criminal client?

Reflection Questions: Wrap-Up for Business Professionals

1. You are a business person who is hosting potential foreign business partners for your company. Consider how you will prepare for their visit.
2. Your company has set up an office in Nairobi, Kenya. You are being sent to that office for two years. Think about how you will prepare for living in that country.
3. Think about how you would set up an advertising campaign for your car company for Brazil. Japan? India?
4. You are on a business trip in Russia. You hear someone say a word in Russian that sounds offense in your native language. What do you do?
5. You are being sent to manage your company's office in Egypt. Think about what you will need to do to manage the workforce there.

Conclusion

In an article on teaching clinical students cultural skills, Professor Antoinette Sedillo López tells the story of how cultural beliefs can affect a bankruptcy case.[186] A Navajo family, who lived in a mobile home, was in danger of losing that home because the husband had lost his job. Accordingly, a clinical student prepared bankruptcy papers for the family. In disclosing their property, the family discussed "in great detail the quantity and quality of a Pendleton and woven blankets they own[ed]." However, they did not disclose any vehicles or livestock.

Finding this strange, the student and supervisor contacted experts on Navajo law. They discovered that "In Navajo culture, blankets are an indicator of wealth and status. The Pendleton and woven blankets are very important to the family and the knowledge that they are more than likely going to keep them upon declaring bankruptcy would be very reassuring." Moreover, "in Navajo culture, livestock could be owned by some family members, but used by others. Thus, the family could be correct in not listing the horses as part of the bankruptcy estate. This is very important, because if the horses do belong to them, even in part, they must list them on the bankruptcy petition, or risk the loss of the ability to discharge their debts." Finally, "As for the vehicle in which the family arrived for interviews, it is common for many Navajo families who live on reservations to borrow vehicles from other families, and it is also possible that the vehicles might be shared."

This story illustrates the importance of cultural competence for lawyers and others interacting with persons from other cultures. This skill will not only help your clients, but they will help your career.

Notes

1. Neil Hamilton & Jeff Maleska, *Helping Students Develop Affirmative Evidence of Cross-Cultural Competency*, 19 THE SCHOLAR: ST. MARY'S L. REV. in RACIAL AND SOCIAL JUSTICE 187, 191 (2017).

2. Susan Bryant, *The Five Habits: Cross-Cultural Competence in Lawyers*, 8 Clinical Law Review 33, 57 (2001).

3. *Id.*

4. Louise Rasmussen, *Cross-Cultural Competence: Engage People from any Culture*, Global Cognition (July 14, 2020). [https://www.globalcognition.org/cross-cultural-competence/]. *See also* Sylvia Stevens, *Cultural Competency, Is There an Ethical Duty*, OREGON STATE BAR BULLETIN, (Jan. 2009) ("Cultural competency is the ability to adapt, work and manage successfully in new and unfamiliar cultural settings."). [https://www.osbar.org/publications/bulletin/09jan/barcounsel.html]

5. James P. Johnson et.al., *Cross-cultural competence in international business: toward a definition and a model*, 37 J. OF INTERNATIONAL BUSINESS STUDIES 525, 527 (2006). https://citeseerx.ist.psu.edu/viewdoc/download?doi=10.1.1.954.3031&rep=rep1&type=pdf]

6. *Id.* at 529.

7. Stevens, *supra.*

8. Mary A. Lynch et al., Intercultural Effectiveness, in Building on Best Practices: Transforming Legal Education in a Changing World 339 (Deborah Maranville et al. eds., 2015).

9. Stevens, *supra*; *see also* Bryant, *supra* at 38 (2001).

10. The Council of the Section of Legal Education and Admissions to the Bar of the American Bar Association recently proposed that cross-cultural competence become a part of the law school curriculum. [https://www.americanbar.org/content/dam/aba/administrative/legal_education_and_admissions_to_the_bar/council_reports_and_resolutions/comments/2021/21-may-notice-and-comment-standards-205-206-303-507-508.pdf] They did not define cross-cultural competence. As of the date of the publication of this book, cultural competence is an optional skill in legal education. Interpretation 302-1 [https://www.americanbar.com/content/dam/aba/administrative/legal_education_and_admissions_to_the_bar/standards/2020-2021/2020-21-aba-standards-and-rules-chapter3.pdf]

11. Stevens, *supra.*

12. https://www.americanbar.org/groups/professional_responsibility/publications/model_rules_of_professional_conduct/rule_1_1_competence/.

13. Johnson et.al., *supra* at 525 ("Business practitioners who are otherwise successful in their domestic markets may struggle and fail in the international business environment when cultural differences are at stake, because of their low level of CC.").

14. *Id.*

15. Neal Goodman, *Training for cultural competence*, 44 INDUSTRIAL & COMMERCIAL TRAINING, 47, 47 (2012). [https://www.emerald.com/insight/content/doi/10.1108/00197851211193426/full/html]

16. Bryant, *supra* at 40.

17. Hamilton & Maleska, *supra* at 201.

18. Louise Rasmussen, *7 Habits of Cross-Cultural Experts*, Global Cognition (July 15, 2020). [https://www.globalcognition.org/7-habits-of-cross-cultural-experts/]

19. Sarah S. Willen et.al., *Opening Up a Huge Can of Worms: Reflections on a "Cultural Sensitivity" Course for Psychiatry Residents*, 18 HARV REV PSYCHIATRY 247 (2010). [DOI: 10.3109/10673229.2010.493748]

20. *Id.* at 251; *see also* Mary Kate Worsin & Nassima Ait-Daoud Tiouririne, *Cultural competence and curricular design: learning the hard way*, 7 PERSPECTIVES ON MEDICAL EDUCATION 8 (2018). [https://link.springer.com/article/10.1007/s40037-018-0428-7].

21. Sarah S, Willen, *Confronting a "Big Huge Gaping Wound": Emotion and Anxiety in a Cultural Sensitivity Course for Psychiatry Residents*, 37 CULTURE, MEDICINE, AND PSYCHIATRY 253 (2013). [HTTPS://LINK.SPRINGER.COM/ARTICLE/10.1007/S11013-013-9310-6]

22. Amanda Gaid, *Using Your Interpersonal Skills to Improve Your Home and Work Life*, BERLO (Jan. 1, 2021) [https://www.oberlo.com/blog/interpersonal-skills]; *Skills You Need: Interpersonal Skills*. [https://www.skillsyouneed.com/interpersonal-skills.html]; Jesal Shethna, *10 Excellent Ways to Develop Interpersonal Skills at Work*, EDUCBA. [https://www.educba.com/ how-to-develop-interpersonal-skills-at-work/].

23. Kendra Cherry, *Understanding Body Language and Facial Expressions*, VERYWELLMIND (SEPT. 28, 2019). [https://www.verywellmind.com/understand-body-language-and-facial-expressions-4147228]; *Body Language Beyond Words – How to Read Unspoken Signals*, [https://www.mindtools.com/pages/article/Body_Language.htm].

24. Starla Sireno, *How To Deal With Difficult People In The Workplace*, Forbes (May 9, 2019). [https://www.forbes.com/sites/forbescoachescouncil/2019/05/09/how-to-deal-with-difficult-people-in-the-workplace/?sh=736e90ec5781]

25. Mat Apodaca, How to Deal with Difficult People: 10 Expert Techniques, LIFE HACK. [https://www.lifehack.org/articles/communication/how-deal-with-difficult-people.html]; Harish Saras, *22 Smart Techniques to Deal with Difficult People at Work*. [https://www.harishsaras.com/stress-management/how-to-deal-with-difficult-people-at-work/]

26. SUSAN A. AMBROSE ET.AL., HOW LEARNING WORKS: 7 RESEARCH-BASED PRINCIPLES FOR SMART TEACHING 68 (2010).

27. DUANE F. SHELL ET.AL., THE UNIFIED LEARNING MODEL: HOW MOTIVATIONAL, COGNITIVE, AND NEUROBIOLOGICAL SCIENCES INFORM BEST TEACHING PRACTICES 14 (2010).

28. *Id.* at 118-121; *see also* AMBROSE, *supra* at 72 (The students truly want to learn.),

29. Judith L. Meece et.al., *Classroom Goal Structure, Student Motivation, and Academic Achievement*, 57 ANN. REV. PSYCH. 487, 490 (2006). [http://tu-dresden.de/die_tu_dresden/fakultaeten/fakultaet_mathematik_und_naturwissenschaften/fachrichtung_psychologie/i4/l ehrlern/lehre/diplom/lehrveranstaltungen/lehren_lernen/annurev.psych.Goal_Meece2005.pdf]

30. SHELL, *supra* at 118; Elizabeth A. Linnenbrink & Paul R. Pintrich, *Motivation as an Enabler for Academic Success*, 31 SCHOOL PSYCH. REV. 313, 320-21 (2002). [http://supadoc.syr.edu/docushare/dsweb/Get/Document-26613/motivationAsEnabler2002.pdf].

31. AMBROSE, *supra* at 71; Shawn M. Glynn et.al., *Motivation to Learn in General Education Programs*, 54 J. GEN. ED. 150, 159 (2005). [http://jesserbishop.wiki.westga.edu/file/view/motivation%20general%20education.pdf].

32. Glynn, *supra* at 159; Paul R. Pintrich, *Motivation and Classroom Learning*, in 2 HAND-BOOK OF PSYCHOLOGY 110 (2003).

33. SHELL, *supra* at 118; Linnenbrink, *supra* at 320-21.

34. AMBROSE, *supra* at 70-82; Pintrich, *supra* at 105.

35. AMBROSE, *supra* at 74; SHELL, *supra* at 70.

36. SHELL, *supra* at 71.

37. AMBROSE, *supra* at 75.

38. *Id.*

39. *Id.*

40. *Id.* at 76-77.

41. *Id.* at 77.

42. *Id.* at 124-126.

43. *Id.* at 125.

44. George M. Slavich & Philip G. Zimbardo, *Transformational Teaching: Theoretical Underpinnings, Basic Principles, and Core Methods*, ED. PSYCH. REV. 560, 578 (2010) [http://ted.coe.wayne.edu/ed7999/Transformational.pdf]; *see also* Albert Bandura & Edwin A. Locke, *Negative Self-Efficacy and Goal Effects Revisited*, 88 J. Applied Psych. 87, 87 (2003). [http://projects.ict.usc.edu/itw/gel/BanduraLockeSE-Goals.pdf]. Self-efficacy is distinguishable from self-esteem in that self-efficacy is situated and contextualized (task specific), while self-esteem is more general. Linnenbrink, *supra* at 315.

45. SHELL, *supra* at 126; *see also* Bandura & Locke, *supra* at 87 ("Whatever other factors serve as guides and motivators, they are rooted in the core belief that one has the power to produce

desired effects; otherwise, one has little incentive to act or to persevere in the face of difficulties.").

46. Linnenbink, *supra* at 315.

47. SHELL, *supra* at 127; Glynn, *supra* at 161.

48. AMBROSE, *supra* at 78.

49. Slavich & Zimbardo, *supra* at 578; SHELL, *supra* at 127.

50. Michael Hunter Schwartz, *Teaching Law Students to be Self-Regulated Learners*, 2003 MICH. ST. DCL L. REV. 447, 456 (2003).

51. SHELL, *supra* at 76

52. *Id.*

53. *Id.* at 77.

54. SHELL, *supra* at 78-80; *see also* Linnenbrink, *supra* at 318 ("interest in general is defined as the interaction between the individual and his or her environment.").

55. SHELL, *supra* at 78-79; Glynn, *supra* at 155; Linnenbrink, *supra* at 319.

56. *Id.* at 80; Glynn, *supra* at 155 ("Students . . . who are interested or curious about topics are oriented toward inquiry and discovery. . ."); Linnenbrink, *supra* at 319.

57. SHELL, *supra* at 80.

58. https://www.nytimes.com/2019/10/18/opinion/sunday/curiositybrain.html?action=click&module=Opinion&pgtype=Homepage.

59. Linnenbrink, *supra* at 317.

60. *Id.*

61. *Id.*

62. Slavich & Zimbardo, *supra* at 579.

63. *See also id.* at 589. This has also been phrased in terms of whether a student has control over his or her learning. Pintrich, *supra* at 106 ("This self-determination perspective is crucial in intrinsic motivation theories of motivation in which students are only intrinsically motivated if they feel autonomous and their behavior is self-determined rather than controlled by others.").

64. Linnenbrink, *supra* at 321.

65. Slavich & Zimbardo, *supra* at 588.

66. Christopher A. Wolters, *Regulation of Motivation: Evaluating an Underemphasized Aspect of Self-Regulated Learning*, 38 EDUC. PSYCH. 189, 199 (2003). [http://faculty.coe.uh.edu/cwolters/docs/walters%282003%29-edpsych.pdf]

67. The Telegraph, *You can do it! Scientists find urging yourself on in the second person is the key to sporting success.* [https://www.telegraph.co.uk/science/2019/07/09/can-do-scientists-find-urging-second-person-key-sporting-success/]

68. AMBROSE, *supra* at 89.

69. Barry J. Zimmerman, *Becoming a Self-Regulated Learner: An Overview*, 41 THEORY INTO PRACTICE 64, 68-69 (2002).

70. Wolters, *supra* at 194.

71. *Id.*

72. *Id.*

73. *Id.* at 195.

74. *Id.*

75. *Id.*

76. *Id.* at 196.

77. *Id.*

78. *Id.*

79. *Id.*

80. *Id.* at 199-200.

81. *Id.* at 200.

82. Bryant, *supra* at 43.

83. Adam B. Cohen, *Many Forms of Culture*, 64 AMERICAN PSYCHOLOGIST 194, 195 (May 2009) [DOI: 10.1037/a0015308]

84. Danielle Tully, *The Culture (Re)Turn: The Case for Teaching Culturally Responsive Lawyering*, 15 STANFORD Journal of Civil Rights & Civil Liberties 201, 209 (2020).

85. M. H. Degall et.al., *Cross-cultural psychology as a scholarly discipline: On the flowering of culture in behavioral research*, 53 AMERICAN PSYCHOLOGIST 1101, 1104 (1998).

86. Cohen, *supra* at 200.

87. Bindu Pillai, *Cultural Barriers*, in INTERNATIONAL MEDICAL GRADUATES IN THE UNITED STATES 118 (2021).

88. *Id.* at 119-20.

89. Bryant, *supra* at 45-46.

90. *Id.* at 43-45.

91. *Id.* at 53.

92. Sophie Thompson, *Cultural Differences in Body Language to be Aware of*, (Aug. 25, 2017). [https://virtualspeech.com/blog/cultural-differences-in-body-language]

93. *Id.*

94. *Id.*

95. Pillai, *supra* at 118.

96. Thompson, *supra*.

97. Pillai, *supra* at 119,

98. Thompson, *supra*.

99. David Matsumoto, *American-Japanese Cultural Differences in the Recognition of Universal Facial Expressions*, 23 JOURNAL OF CROSS-CULTURAL PSYCHOLOGY 72 (1992). [http://matsumotogroup.com/content/1992%20American%20Japanese%20Cultural%20Differences.pdf]

100. Alan S. Cowen et.al., *Sixteen facial expressions occur in similar contexts worldwide*, 589 NATURE 251 (2021). [https://www.nature.com/articles/s41586-020-3037-7]

101. Nalini Tarakeshwar et.al, Religion: *An Overlooked Dimension in Cross-Cultural Psychology*, 34 JOURNAL OF CROSS-CULTURAL PSYCHOLOGY 377 (2003). [http://jc.com/cgi/content/abstract/34/4/377]

102. *Id.*

103. *Id.* at 378.

104. Cohen, *supra* at 198 (May 2009). [DOI: 10.1037/a0015308]

105. *Id.*

106. *Id.* at 198.

107. *Id.* at 197.

108. *Id.*

109. *Id.* at 198.

110. Arnold R. Eiser & Glenn Ellis, *Viewpoint: Cultural Competence and the African American Experience with Health Care: The Case for Specific Content in Cross-Cultural Education*, 82 Academic Medicine 176, 177 (2007).

111. *Id.*

112. *Id.*

113. *Id.* at 179.

114. Bryant, *supra* at 51.

115. *Id.* at 67.

116. Roy Stuckey et.al., Best Practices for Legal Education: A Vision and a Roadmap 39 (2007).

117. *Id.* at 66.

118. Sue Bryant & Jean Koh Peters, *Five Habits of Cross-Cultural Lawyering*. [https://fivehabitsandmore.law.yale.edu/jean-and-sues-materials/habits/]

119. Knowledge@Wharton, *Is Your Team Culturally Competent?* (June 20, 2019). [https://knowledge.wharton.upenn.edu/article/companies-cultural-competency/]

120. Tully, *supra* at 209-10.

121. Bryant, *supra* at 42.

122. Carina Weng, *Multicultural Lawyering: Teaching Psychology to Develop Cultural Self-Awareness*, 11 CLINICAL LAW REVIEW 369 (2004-2005) at 7-8. [http://ssrn.com/abstract=704023] (Pagination from SSRN version)

123. *Id.* at 10.

124. *Id.* at 11-12.

125. *Id.* at 18.

126. Weng, *supra* at 19.

127. Paul R. Tremblay, *Interviewing and Counseling Across Cultures: Heuristics and Biases*, 9 CLINICAL LAW REVIEW 373 390 (2002).

128. *Id.* at 22.

129. Hamilton and Maleska believe that "empathy is at the heart of developing cross-cultural competency for students and lawyers." Hamilton & Maleska, *supra* at 190.

130. *Wikipedia: Empathy*. [https://en.wikipedia.org/wiki/Empathy]

131. Hamilton & Maleska, *supra* at 205.

132. John L. Barkai, *How to Develop the Skill of Active Listening*, http://papers.ssrn.com/sol3/papers.cfm?abstract_id=1437265 at 73.

133. Hamilton & Maleska, *supra* at 19.

134. Bryant, *supra* at 56 ("Remaining non-judgmental is a core cross-cultural skill and one that is particularly difficult for lawyers.").

135. JENNIFER YORK-BARR ET.AL., REFLECTIVE PRACTICE TO IMPROVE SCHOOLS: AN ACTION GUIDE FOR EDUCATORS 4 (2006).

136. Marian Murphy et.al., *Reflective Inquiry in Social Work Education*, in Handbook of Reflection and Reflective Inquiry: Mapping a Way of Knowing for Professional Reflective Inquiry 177 (2010).

137. P. J. Feltovich et. al, *Studies of Expertise from Psychological Perspectives*, in The Cambridge Handbook of Expertise and Expert Performance 55 (K. Anders Ericsson et. al. eds., 2006).

138. Just Write Guide, 41. [https://lincs.ed.gov/sites/default/files/TEAL_JustWriteGuide.pdf]

139. Anthony S. Niedwiecki, *Lawyers and Learning: A Metacognitive Approach to Legal Education*, 13 Widener L. Rev. 33, 42-43 (2006).

140. Just Write Guide, *supra* at 32.

141. Brain storming is a problem-solving technique. With brain storming, you think of as many ideas as possible to solve a problem without being critical of your ideas. When you are done, you critically pick out the ideas you think will work.

142. For more on critical thinking, *see* E. SCOTT FRUEHWALD, HOW TO TEACH LAWYERS, JUDGES, AND LAW STUDENTS CRITICAL THINKING: MILLIONS SAW THE APPLE FALL, BUT NEWTON ASKED WHY (2020).

143. Daniel T. Willingham, *Critical Thinking: Why Is It So Hard to Teach?* 109 ARTS EDUCATION POLICY REVIEW 21, 22 (2008). Willingham, *supra* at 22.

144. Tanju Deveci & Nader Ayich, Correlation between Critical Thinking and Lifelong Learning Skills of Freshman Students, https://dergipark.org.tr/en/download/article-file/275667 at 284 (2007). The Stanford Encyclopedia of Philosophy: Critical Thinking notes that critical thinking's "definition is contested, but the competing definitions can be understood as differing conceptions of the same basic concept: careful thinking directed to a goal." [https://plato.stanford.edu/entries/critical-thinking/ (2018).]

145. Adam M. Persky et.al., *Developing Critical Thinking Skills in Pharmacy Students*, 83 AMERICAN JOURNAL OF PHARMACEUTICAL EDUCATION 161, 161 (2019).

146. Dana S. Dunn, Jane S. Halonen, and Randolph A. Smith, *Preface*, in TEACHING CRITICAL THINKING IN PSYCHOLOGY: A HANDBOOK OF BEST PRACTICES xvii (2008).

147. James P. Byrnes & Kevin N. Dunbar, *The Nature and Development of Critical-Analytic Thinking*, 26 EDUC. PSYCHOL. REV. 477, 478-79 (2014).

148. Willingham, *supra* at 27 (2008).

149. Byrnes & Dunbar, *supra* at 480-81; *see also* Tim Van Gelder, Teaching Critical Thinking: Some lessons from Cognitive Science, 53 COLLEGE TEACHING 41 (2005).

150. https://dictionary.cambridge.org/us/dictionary/english/assumption.

151. Jennifer Wilson Mulnix, *Thinking Critically about Critical Thinking*, EDUCATIONAL PHILOSOPHY & THEORY 11 (2010); Van Gelder, *supra* at 42.

152. Mulnix, *supra* at 11.

153. Van Gelder, *supra* at 42.

154. Eugene Volokh, *Zero correlation between state homicide rate and state gun laws,* Washington Post (Oct. 6, 2015) [https://www.washingtonpost.com/news/volokh-conspiracy/wp/2015/10/06/zero-correlation-between-state-homicide-rate-and-state-gun-laws/?utm_term=.561a19c24711]

155. "Research in expertise has confirmed that reorganization and transformation of a problem until a known solution is found is what distinguishes expert from non-expert problem solving.... Working memory processing recombines existing retrieved knowledge [from long-term memory] and sensory input until it finds an adequate resolution for the problem or accomplishes the task." SHELL, *supra* at 54.

156. Byrnes & Dunbar, *supra* at 479.

157. *Id.*

158. *Id.*

159. Katherine Schulten, *Skills and Strategies | Making Inferences*, THE NEW YORK TIMES (Sept. 2, 2015) [https://learning.blogs.nytimes.com/2015/09/02/skills-and-strategies-making-inferences/]

160. *Id.*

161. Mulnix, *supra* at 10.

162. *Id.*

163. Peter Lipton, Inference to the Best Explanation 5 (2004).

164. Bradley J. Charles, Applying Law 41 (2011).

165. For more on cognitive biases, see E. Scott Fruehwald, Understanding and Over-coming Cognitive Biases For Lawyers And Law Students: Becoming a Better Lawyer Through Cognitive Science (2018).

166. Kendra Cherry, *What is a Cognitive Bias? Defintions and Examples*, VeryWell (May 26, 2016). [https://www.verywell.com/what-is-a-cognitive-bias-2794963] *See also* Daniel Kahneman, Thinking, Fast and Slow (2011).

167. David Z. Hambrick & Alexander P. Burgoyne, *The Difference Between Rationality and Intelligence*, N.Y. Times (Sept. 16, 2016) [http://www.nytimes.com/2016/09/18/_opinion/sunday/the-difference-between-rationalityandintelligence.html?rref=collection%2Fcolumn%2FGray%20Matter&action=click&contentCollection=Opinion&module=Collection&region=Marginalia&src=me&version=column&pgtype=article&_r=1

168. Kahneman, *supra* at 13-14.

169. Philip Fernbach & Steven Sloman, *Why We Believe Obvious Untruths*, New York Times (March 3, 2017). [https://www.nytimes.com/2017/03/03/opinion/sunday/why-we-believe-obvious-untruths.html?_r=0]

170. Irene Scopelliti et.al., *Bias Blind Spot: Structure, Measurement, and Consequences*, 61 Management Science 2468 (2015) (The intensity of the bias does vary anong individuals.). [https://pubsonline.informs.org/doi/abs/10.1287/mnsc.2014.2096] *See also* Kathleen A. Tomlin et.al., *Are Students Blind to Their Ethical Blind Spots? An Exploration of Why Ethics Education Should Focus on Self-Perception Biases*, 41 Journal of Management Education 539 (2017). [https://doi.org/10.1177/1052562917701500]

171. Scopelliti, *supra*.

172. *Id.* at 57.

173. *E.g.*, Greg Lukianoff and Jonathan Haidt, The Coddling of the American Mind, The Atlantic (Sept 15 2015). [http://www.theatlantic.com/magazine/archive/2015/09/]; Hambrick & Burgoyne, *supra*; Carey K. Morewedge et.al., Debiasing Decisions: Improved Decision Making With a Single Training Intervention, 2 Policy Insights from the Behavioral and Brain Sciences 129–140 (2015).

174. Raymond S. Nickerson, *Confirmation Bias: A Ubiquitous Phenomenon in Many Guises*, 2 Review of General Psychology 175, 175 (1998). [http://landman-psychology.com/ConfirmationBias.pdf]

175. SHRM, *Intercultural Competence as a Key Enabler of Organizational Growth and Success*, [https://www.shrm.org/resourcesandtools/tools-and-samples/toolkits/pages/interculturalcompetence.aspx].

176. *Id.*

177. Melissa Lamson, *10 Tips To Develop Your Firm's Cultural Competence*, INC. [https://www.inc.com/melissa-lamson/cultural-competence-your-most-valuable-business-asset.html]

178. Jane Hyun and Douglas Conant, *3 Ways to Improve Your Cultural Fluency* (April 25, 2019). [https://hbr.org/2019/04/3-ways-to-improve-your-cultural-fluency]

179. Knowledge@Wharton, *supra*.

180. Dr. Richard Nongard, *6 Ways Businesses Benefit From Cultural Competence*, (Aug. 20, 2018).

181. *Id.*

182. *How Lack of Cultural Awareness Can Cost A Business Big.* [https://www.commisceo-global.com/blog/cultural-sensitivity-in-business-1]

183. ARC Business Solutions, *What Small Business Owners Should Know About Cultural Competence in Marketing*. [https://www.arcanswers.com/small-business/what-small-business-owners- should-know-about-cultural-competence-in-marketing/]

184. *Id.*

185. Tatenda Sayenda, *Cultural Competence: Everything You Need Know*, (Nov. 3, 2020). [https://www.thehumancapitalhub.com/articles/Cultural-Competence--Everything-You-Need-Know]

186. Antoinette Sedillo López, *Making and Breaking Habits: Teaching (and Learning) Cultural Context, Self-Awareness, and Intercultural Communication Context, Self-Awareness, and Intercultural Communication Through Case Supervision in a Client-Service Legal Clinic Through Case Supervision in a Client-Service Legal Clinic*, 28 Wash. U. J. L. & Pol'y 37 (2008).

www.ingramcontent.com/pod-product-compliance
Lightning Source LLC
Chambersburg PA
CBHW070455220526
45466CB00004B/1833